LETTERS TO LOUISE

The Answers Are Within You

Louise L. Hay

Hodder & Stoughton

Copyright © 1998 by Louise L. Hay

The right of Louise L. Hay to be identified as the Author of the Work has been asserted by her in accordance with the Copyright, Designs and Patents Act 1988.

First published in Great Britain in 1999 by Hodder & Stoughton A division of Hodder Headline PLC

10 9 8 7 6 5 4 3 2 1

British Library Cataloguing in Publication Data

A CIP catalogue record for this title is available from the British Library

ISBN 0 340 70729 1

Typeset by Hewer Text Ltd, Edinburgh Printed and bound in Great Britain by Clays Ltd, St Ives PLC

Hodder and Stoughton A division of Hodder Headline PLC 338 Euston Road London NW1 3BH

LETTERS TO LOUISE

CONTENTS

APPENDICES

INTRODUCTION

by Louise L. Hay

This book is a collection of letters I've received and answered over the years from people all over the world. The letters express deep concerns about many areas of life. Almost all of the people who have written to me have wanted to change themselves – and their world – in some way. In my replies, I have tried to be the catalyst that helps these individuals accomplish their goals. I think of myself as a stepping-stone on a pathway of self-discovery. I create a space where people can learn how wonderful they are by teaching them to love themselves. That's all I do. I'm not a healer. I'm a person who supports people. I help them discover their own power and inner wisdom and strengths, and I help them get the blocks and the barriers out of the way so they can love themselves no matter what their circumstances.

Perhaps you will see some aspect of yourself in these pages. It is my belief that by reading about other people's challenges and aspirations, we can see ourselves and our own problems in different ways. Sometimes we can use what we learn from others to make changes in our own lives. I hope this book will allow you to realize that you, too, have the strength within to change, and to find solutions on your own – that is, to seek the answers that 'are within you.'

Some of the ways to find the solutions within are through tools such as affirmations, mirror work, and visualization.

For those of you who are not familiar with the benefits of positive affirmations, I would like to explain a little about them. An affirmation is really anything you say or think. A lot of what we normally say and think is quite negative and does not create good experiences for us. We have to re-train our thinking and speaking into positive patterns if we want to change our lives.

When we talk about 'doing' affirmations, we mean that we make a positive statement about something we want to change in our lives. Too often we say, 'I don't want this in my life,' and we forget to state clearly what we do want. To say, 'I don't want to be sick anymore' does not give the body a clear picture of the health we would like to enjoy. Nor does saying 'I hate this job' produce a great new position. To create the new experiences we want, we need to clearly declare our desires.

Affirmations are like planting seeds in the ground. First they germinate, then they sprout roots, and then they shoot up through the ground. It takes some time to go from a seed to a full-grown plant. And so with affirmations, it takes some time from the first declaration to the final demonstration. So be patient.

Mirror work is another valuable tool. Mirrors reflect the feelings we have about ourselves. They clearly show us the areas that need to be changed if we want a joyous, fulfilling life. The most powerful way to do affirmations is to look in a mirror and say them out loud. I ask people to look in their own eyes and say something positive about themselves every time they pass a mirror. They are immediately aware of any resistance and can move through it quicker.

Visualization is the process of using the imagination to achieve a desired result. Put most simply, you see what you want to happen, before it actually does happen. For example, if what you want is a new place to live, picture a house or an apartment that you want, being as specific as possible. Then see it as if it were already true. Affirm that you deserve it. See your new home with you in it going about your daily routine. Imagine this as clearly as you can, knowing that there is no wrong way to visualize. Practice your visualization frequently, turning all results over to the Universal Mind, and asking for your highest good. Combined with positive affirmations, visualization is a powerful tool.

Remember that through affirmations, mirror work, and visualization, we can come to realize that the answers really *are* within us.

I have arranged the letters in this book by categories (listed alphabetically) such as addictions, death/grief, family issues, fears, relationships, and so forth. Each category is a chapter, and there are 20 chapters in all. Each chapter begins with a meditation and ends with affirmations to help you find your inner strength. At the end of the book, you will find a Recommended Reading list and Self-Help Resources for further growth and exploration.

The past has no power over me because I am willing to learn and to change. I see the past as necessary to bring me to where I am today. I am willing to begin where I am right now to clean the rooms of my mental house. I know it does not matter where I start, so I now begin with the smallest and easiest rooms, and in that way I will see results quickly. I close the door on old hurts and old self-righteous unforgiveness. I visualize a stream before me, and I take the old, hurtful experiences and put them in the stream and see them begin to dissolve and drift downstream until they dissipate and disappear. I have the ability to let go. I am now free. To create anew.

Chapter One

ABUSE

Many of us come from dysfunctional homes. We carry over a lot of negative feelings about who we are and our relationship to life. Our childhood may have been filled with abuse, and perhaps that abuse has continued into our adult lives. When we learn early about fear and abuse, we often continue to re-create those experiences as we grow up. We may be harsh with ourselves, interpreting the lack of love and affection to mean that we are bad and deserve such abuse.

We need to realize that we have the power to change all of this. All the events we have experienced in our lifetime up to the present moment have been created by our thoughts and beliefs from the past. We do not want to look back on our lives with shame. We want to look at the past as part of the richness and fullness of life. Without this richness and fullness, we would not be here today. There is no reason to beat ourselves up because we didn't do better. We did the best we knew how. We often survived dreadful circumstances. We now can release the past in love and be grateful that it has brought us to this new awareness.

The past only exists in our minds and in the way we choose to look at it in our minds. This is the moment we are living. This is the moment we are feeling. This is the moment we are experiencing. What we are doing right now is laying the groundwork for tomorrow. So this is the moment to make the decision. We can't do anything tomorrow, and we can't do it yesterday. We can only do it today. What is important is what we are choosing to think, believe, and say right now.

Louise L. Hay

As we learn to love ourselves and trust our higher Power, we become co-creators with the Infinite Spirit of a loving world. Our love for ourselves moves us from being victims to being winners. Our love for ourselves attracts wonderful experiences to us.

The following letters relate to the topic of abuse:

Dear Louise
My father was an alcoholic, and I endured a lot of mental and physical abuse. At 16 I became pregnant by a boy who treated me badly. His parents arranged for me to go to a home for unwed mothers, which was like being in prison.
A little piece of me broke off in that home. Maybe it was all of the lies that I had to tell my friends and family about where I was going. Maybe it was the unbearable hurt of feeling like no one really loved me or would ever care. Maybe it was feeling like a wimp because I couldn't walk out of there with my baby, like some of the other girls did. Whatever it was, I stopped being able to look people in the eye. I have been to many therapists to get over this pain, but nothing has had an impact on me as much as your book You Can Heal Your Life.
Though I'm just getting started, I've already put your affirmations on cards and have taken them to work. Still, my life seems very painful. I know I have suffered a lot of painful feelings, but it's a hard cycle to break. As a consequence of all the stress I've been under, my hair is beginning to thin. This has upset me tremendously. I've been doing affirmations for that, but I feel a lot of resistance.
Louise, for the first time, I know that my thought processes have to change. I don't want to live my life the way I have in the past.

2

Dear One,

Many of us were mistreated as children and grew up with a negative view about life (I was an abused child, too). We are often afraid of feeling good about ourselves because this is a totally unfamiliar space. I know that people who have been battered and abused feel lots of anger and resentment. They usually have low self-esteem and do not feel 'good enough.' As a result, there are certain things you have acted out in your life with little or no understanding of their roots.

It is time to forgive yourself. The greater intelligence of the universe, that which I believe to be God, has already forgiven you; now it's your turn. We are all magnificent in the sight of God. You can choose to stop punishing yourself, or you can continue to feel like a victim of circumstances. Affirm right now: I LET GO OF THE NEGATIVE EVENTS OF THE PAST. I AM WORTHY OF HAVING PEACE OF MIND AND HEALTHY RELATIONSHIPS. I CREATE LOVING EXPERIENCES IN MY LIFE EACH DAY. Tell yourself, 'I let go,' every time you feel the pain and the guilt. And follow that with 'I am healing this very moment.'

As you establish a habit of saying these things every time you cannot look someone in the eye or when you cannot tell yourself that you love yourself or when you feel like a 'bad' person or when you are not feeling loved or even recognized for the special person you really are, you will begin to show a tremendous difference in your self-esteem.

Remember, though, you must be consistent with this work in order for the subconscious to pick up on these new messages. There may also be a lot of resistance (some of which you are already experiencing). That's okay. It is only fear trying to protect you. It may take you some time to reassure yourself.

Dear Louise,

My sister and I were physically and emotionally abused and neglected as children. As a result of this, I rejected my parents as role models early on and looked to other families for guidelines. However, old memories still haunt me, and now I have more nightmares about my mom than ever. I feel like there's tons of emotional pain deep inside me that keeps seeping out, and someday the dam will break and so much pain will flow forth I'll be drowned.

Should I just tell my parents that I don't want any contact between us anymore? I really don't wish them any suffering, but I wish I would never have to see or hear from them again, and I want the pain to go away.

Dear One,

Rejecting your parents for the time being is probably a good thing for you to do. It seems that the only way they can cope with their guilt is to go into denial. You are not here to heal them; you are here to heal yourself. You can drop them simple notes from time to time.

To begin your own healing, I think it would be a good idea to write your parents a letter, spilling out everything from deep down in your gut. End it by saying, 'It is time for me to heal and to learn to love myself.' Then, burn it and visualize all of the resentment and hurt going with it.

However, this alone will never make all the pain go away. Do connect with a practitioner or call Al-Anon on 0171 403 0888. Al-Anon programs can help in many areas, even if alcohol was not the primary source of abuse. Help is all around you. Reach out for it and know that the Universe is ready to help as soon as you ask. Affirm: I AM READY TO BE HEALED. I AM WILLING TO FORGIVE.

Dear Louise,

I hope you can help me out. My husband is very abusive, physically and mentally. He treats me like a maid and is always yelling at me and making unreasonable demands. He has been diagnosed with cancer and is taking radiation. My daughter overcame drugs and is getting her life back on track, but her nerves are very bad. I am also responsible for my adopted grandson's tuition in ministerial school, and I am afraid this financial responsibility is going to drain me.

I feel overwhelmed. Can you help me deal with everything on my plate?

Dear One,

Of course you are overwhelmed. For goodness' sake, dump your plate, and take a vacation! Get away from all of them while you sort out your priorities. This is your life. No one can abuse you or take advantage of you without your permission. Where is the love you once had for yourself?

All positive changes begin in consciousness. I, too, was taught as a child to walk two steps behind a man and to look up and ask, 'What do I think, and what do I do?' I was also taught to accept abuse as normal. It took me a long time to realize that this behavior was not normal, nor was it what I as a woman deserved. As I slowly began to change my belief system, to change my consciousness, I began to develop self-worth and self-esteem. As I did, my world changed.

Your world can change, too. You need help in changing yourself. Get some counseling. Join Al-Anon. Consult your telephone directory, and call a counseling center or help line near you. Affirm: I NOW CREATE A LOVING WORLD WITHIN MY MIND.

Louise L. Hay

Dear Louise,

Behind the smile that I wear so well at 52 years young lies a beautiful child who has been locked up and buried so deep that even after three years of therapy, she still has not allowed anyone to see her.

I know I was a victim of incest by my natural father for years, and this has caused me to be self-defeating and self-destructive. But when does it end? My therapist has had no luck with me, and I've been told that I have to get to the core of the issue to feel and to heal, but nothing comes through. I'm so confused and unhappy — my physical world is in chaos. I am unemployed now and cannot afford therapy. Can you help me find out who I really am?

Dear One,

At the depth of your pain is a deep unwillingness to forgive. I recognize that your childhood was difficult; yet, for you to hold on to pain is self-defeating. The door to the heart opens inward, and you cannot love yourself until you are willing to let go. You have great inner strength. You have proven it by how strongly you have resisted your therapist. Your father abused your inner child once, and now you are continuing the pattern of abuse.

You have already had three years of therapy, so you know what goes on there. Now it is time for you to use those exercises and insights to heal your own inner child. No therapist can move into healing. Work with the affirmation, I AM WILLING TO FORGIVE AND SET MYSELF FREE, for at least a month. Say it at least 50 times a day. You are powerful, and you can heal. Go for it.

Dear Louise,

I especially love your affirmation: 'I know that everything

happens at exactly the right time for exactly the right reason.
I make the best of every challenge that life places in my path.
All is well.' But tell me, Louise, how do I apply this to my life
when my husband drinks too much and abuses me? I would
love to just tell myself, 'All is well,' but it is not. How can I
make it well? I am 69, and he is 77.

Dear One,
   You do not have to allow anyone to abuse you. We women have endured abuse for generations because we've accepted the belief that we were second-class citizens. I was raised to believe that it was normal for a man to be abusive. It was not until I raised my own self-esteem that abusive men were no longer attracted to me. It is time for all women to find their own inner self-worth and self-esteem. When we do, we will never again allow ourselves to be abused and humiliated.
   Making the best of a challenge can also mean removing yourself from nonsupportive situations. Get out of the house! You are not too old. I am 71, and I don't even feel middle-aged yet. To me, the new middle age is 75. So you still have a great deal of your life before you. Almost every city has centers for abused women. Go and get some help. If your husband will not get help, you can go to Al-Anon or Co-Dependency meetings to learn how to take care of yourself.
   Remember: 'This is the first day of the rest of your life.' Make the most of it. It will be best for both of you. Affirm: I DESERVE LOVE AND PROTECTION, AND I GIVE IT TO MYSELF.

Affirmations for Overcoming Abuse

I release the past and allow time
to heal every area of my life.

I forgive others, I forgive myself,
and I am free to love and enjoy life.

I begin now to allow the child inside to
blossom and to know that it is deeply loved.

I deserve to have boundaries and to have them respected.

I am a valued human being.

I am always treated with respect.

I release the need to blame anyone, including myself.

I deserve the best in my life, and I now accept the best.

I free myself and everyone in my life from old past hurts.

I now choose to eliminate all negative
thoughts and see only my own magnificence.

Heavy dependence upon anything outside myself is addiction. I can be addicted to drugs and alcohol, to sex and tobacco; and I can also be addicted to blaming people, to illness, to debt, to being a victim, to being rejected. Yet, I can move beyond these things. Being addicted is giving up my power to a substance or a habit. I can always take my power back. This is the moment I take my power back! I choose to develop the positive habit of knowing that life is here for me. I am willing to forgive myself and move on. I have an eternal spirit that has always been with me, and it is here with me now. I relax and let go, and I remember to breathe as I release old habits and practice positive new ones.

Chapter Two

ADDICTIONS

O ne of the primary ways we mask our fears is through addictions. Addictions suppress the emotions so that we don't feel. However, there are many kinds of addictions besides chemical ones. There are also what I call pattern addictions – patterns we adopt to keep us from being present in our lives. If we don't want to deal with what's in front of us, or if we don't want to be where we are, we have a pattern that keeps us out of touch with our lives. For some people, it is a food addiction or a chemical addiction. There may be a genetic disposition for alcoholism; however, the choice to stay sick is always an individual one. So often when we talk about something being hereditary, it is really the little child's acceptance of the parents' ways of handling fear.

For others there are emotional addictions. You can be addicted to finding fault in people. No matter what happens, you will always find someone to blame. 'It's their fault. They did it to me.'

Maybe you are addicted to running up bills. There are many of you addicted to being in debt; you do everything to keep yourselves over your heads in debt. It doesn't seem to have anything to do with the amount of money you have.

You can be addicted to rejection. Everywhere you go, you attract others who reject you. However, the rejection on the outside is a reflection of your own rejection. If you don't reject yourself, nobody else will either, or if they do, it certainly won't matter to you. Ask yourself, 'What am I not accepting about myself?'

There are plenty of people addicted to illness. They are always catching something or worrying about getting sick. They seem to belong to the 'Illness-of-the-Month Club.'

If you're going to be addicted to anything, why not be addicted to loving yourself? You can be addicted to saying positive affirmations or doing something that is supportive of you.

Addictions come about because we do not know how to love ourselves. We are afraid to explore ourselves, and instead, we use our addiction to run from self-discovery. If we can change how we think about ourselves, we can stop running, learn to love ourselves, and find our power within.

The following letters relate to the topic of addictions:

Dear Louise,

I am 46 and have smoked for over 30 years. Can you say a few words about cigarettes? The whole social climate surrounding smoking these days, especially in California, is uncomfortable. Smokers are forced outside to smoke, but that's not good enough — some people don't even want us to smoke outside now.

I quit drinking and using drugs almost nine years ago, and that was a tremendous thing for me to have done — a total turnaround in my life — and I have never felt better than I do right now. But I smoke cigarettes and enjoy it very much. I know I am being easy on myself about smoking because quitting drinking and drugs was such a big deal.

I admit I'm afraid to go through the psychological trauma associated with stopping such an ingrained habit. I don't think anti-smoking people have any conception of this; they probably think one can 'just say no.'

What I really want is for smoking not to be unhealthy so I can smoke happily for the rest of my life. I want the anti-

smoking people to go find something more meaningful to focus on. And if and when I decide to live without the cigarette habit, I don't want the withdrawal to be traumatic.

Dear One,

First, let me say that I, too, smoked for many years. I began when I was 15 so I could be defiant and grown up. Letting cigarettes go took me a long time. People who smoke are usually unaware that they smell like a dirty ashtray, so at one point, I used to take a deep whiff of the ashtray in the hallway of my apartment building first thing in the morning on my way to work so I would be aware of how I smelled to others. In the end, Life was kind to me. I went to a workshop for a month where no one smoked, nor did I. When I came home, I had half a cigarette and became very ill. I gratefully went to bed and have never had another cigarette.

I imagine releasing alcohol and drugs was difficult for you, yet your life improved. It will improve again when you release smoking. Yet, this is your decision to make. You will do it at the right time, and you may smoke until you leave the planet. I do not see that there is right or wrong involved where only you are concerned. It is your life, and I can't tell you what to do. However, the anti-smoking people have learned that secondhand smoke is very detrimental to non-smokers' health, and they do not want to be around it or smell it.

Let's know and affirm together that *if* you make a decision to quit, it will come easily and effortlessly. Nothing is permanent in life. Smoking came into your life at the right time and will leave at the right time, in the perfect way. A good affirmation for you is: I AM AT PEACE WITH MY LIFE AND WITH OTHERS. ALL IS WELL.

Louise L. Hay

Dear Louise.

I am 37 years old, obese, and I don't know where to turn. I suffer from a long list of addictive/compulsive behaviors. Currently, I am in a hospital for treatment of my bulimia. They want me to work with a 12-step program, but I get frustrated with the program because I have no idea what they want from me. Previously, I attended one group after another, but it would never last.

All I know is that I hurt very deeply inside. I want to turn my addictive/compulsive behavior over to my Higher Power, but I have a hard time accepting that I am responsible for my own life problems. I want to change, but I am afraid.

Dear One,

I can sense your frustration about yourself. Bulimia is often related to self-hatred. There is a feeling of throwing up the self and a feeling of not being worthy. People with bulimia often feel that they will never be loved as they are.

As hard as it may seem, forget about controlling your weight, your intake of food, and about how you look right now. That is a part of the self-rejecting mechanism that's going on with you. Repeat over and over to yourself in a mirror: 'I love you. I really love you.' You know that inside you are a beautiful, divine being, no matter what weight you are.

You say that you have participated in a number of programs and groups with no success. Twelve-step programs are wonderful, and there is no need to be afraid of the work they want you to do, but the work must be continual or else it is ineffective. When you're away from the meeting, do you visualize your life exactly the way you want it to be? Do you sit quietly by yourself to get centered and meditate? Do you do your positive affirmations all the time? A good affirmation for you could be: I ACCEPT MY OWN LOVE, AND I NOW FIND JOY AND PLEASURE IN BEING WHO I AM.

14

I believe the miracle cure that you are looking for will not be found in another program unless you are willing to admit that the solutions to your difficulties are within you. Do the mirror work and begin to get to know yourself. Once you begin to truly appreciate yourself, little miracles will appear everywhere.

Dear Louise,

I am a 22-year-old male with a history of childhood sexual, physical, mental, and emotional abuse. I feel that I have dealt with the anger toward the man who perpetrated this upon me, but I am still keeping the abuse alive by overstepping my body's sexuality.

I am writing this letter because of my 'sexual addiction.' I find that I seek out sexual experiences with one man after another, although I don't really get much pleasure out of it. For a couple of years, I have wanted this behavior to stop, but it just seems as if my mind is not in harmony with this decision.

Dear One,

How wonderful that you are reaching out for help. Ask and ye shall receive. For more information on resources available to you, send an SAE to the National Council on Sexual Addictions and Compulsivity, 1090 S. Northchase Parkway, Suite 200, South Marietta, GA 30067; or call (770) 989–9754. They will be most happy to give you the location of the Sexual Recovery group nearest you.

Treat yourself with love, and know that any negative pattern can be dissolved if you are willing to work on it. You are worth loving, you are lovable. In this day of Aids (I always lower-case the acronym to diminish its importance), do be especially careful both for yourself and for your

partners. A healing affirmation for you could be: I AM
HEALED AND WHOLE IN EVERY AREA OF MY LIFE.

Dear Louise.

  *My childhood was very challenging, to say the least, due to
my parents' drinking. I was never sure which personality I
would come home to – the silly, fun drunk people; or the
frightening, sometimes abusive ones. Needless to say, I very
rarely brought friends home to play.*

  *I bolted from home at age 18, and then my parents finally
started attending AA meetings, enjoying ten years of sobriety.
Our relationship became incredibly close, and I got to know
them as the beautiful, caring people they are.*

  *My problem is this: All of a sudden they've begun to drink
again, and even though I know that they're both on their own
paths and I can't be responsible for them, I still wonder if
there's something I can do or say so that they don't slip back
into that alcohol-induced world. Any words of wisdom?*

Dear One,

  How discouraging for you, and I'm glad that you realize
that it is not *your* problem. We always want what is best for
our parents, and yet it is hard for us to see the larger picture.
We cannot always be aware of what experience is needed by
an individual on a soul level. We know that all of life's
experiences have value. What your parents are going
through has value to them on a soul level. Our parents
are our greatest teachers, and sometimes the lesson they
teach us is 'how not to behave.' Be glad that you did have a
period of ten years of closeness with them to cherish in your
memory. Love them and know that the Intelligence within
them is always available to them at all times.

  If you want help from experts on how to handle the

immediate situation, I would suggest that you go to Al-Anon. It is a wonderful organization and has far more answers than I do. Love yourself, be very kind to your inner child, and affirm: I AM AT PEACE WITH EVERY ASPECT OF MY LIFE.

Dear Louise.

My husband of three years has been smoking pot every night since he got out of college almost two decades ago. At first, I didn't mind that he indulged in what I consider an addiction every night when he came home from work. He holds a good job, and he is not abusive in any way. But more and more, it has started to bother me.

I feel that pot deadens emotions – not allowing a person to really feel anything. Whenever something unpleasant arises, my husband just lights up a joint instead of allowing himself to experience his feelings. I believe that this affects our love life and our level of communication. However, when I've asked him to stop smoking, he has responded, 'You knew who I was when you met me. I'm never going to stop, so you have to make the choice about dealing with it or not.'

My dilemma is: do I just let him be, or do I try to make him see that he really is a drug addict?

Dear One,

WE CANNOT CHANGE OTHER PEOPLE – no matter how much we may feel we know what is best for them! Your husband has never kept secrets from you. You knew of his habits before you married him. When you insist that he stop smoking, you only make his resistance stronger. If you make this into a war, you will only lose. It could even end your marriage. Do you want to go that far? Rather than trying to change him, I would like to suggest that you work on yourself.

It is important that you feel good, and your thoughts determine whether you feel good or not. In the privacy of your own mind, practice your affirmations for the kind of marriage you feel you really want. Be careful that your affirmations only talk about what you *do* want, not what you *don't* want. (Not: 'I don't want my husband to smoke,' but 'I want us both to be very comfortable in this marriage.') Search your thoughts and find those that make you feel good. Find lots of things about your marriage to be grateful for. Love yourself. Appreciate your life. Allow the Universe to flow happiness and joy through you. Affirm: 'I HAVE A WONDERFUL MARRIAGE, AND WE ARE BOTH HAPPY AND FREE!'

Affirmations for Overcoming Addictions

I see any resistance patterns within
me only as something to release.

I am loved and nourished and supported by Life itself.

I am doing the best that I can. Each day gets easier.

I am willing to release the need for my addictions.

I move beyond my addictions and set myself free.

I approve of myself and the way I am changing.

I am more powerful than my addictions.

I now discover how wonderful I am.

I choose to love and enjoy myself.

It is safe for me to be alive.

In the infinity of life where I am, all is perfect, whole, and complete. I no longer choose to believe in the old limitations and lack that once defined the aging process. I rejoice in each passing year. My wealth of knowledge grows, and I am in touch with my wisdom. My later years are my treasure years, and I know how to keep myself youthful and healthy. My body is renewed at every moment. I am vital, vivacious, healthy, fully alive, and contributing to my last day. I now choose to live my life from this understanding. I am at peace with my age.

Chapter Three

AGING

For generations, we have allowed the numbers that correspond to how many years we have been on the planet to tell us how to feel, how to look, and how to behave. As with any other aspect of life, what we mentally accept and believe becomes true for us. Well, it is time to change our beliefs about aging. When I look around and see frail, sick, frightened older people, I say to myself, 'It doesn't have to be that way.' Many of us have learned that by changing our thinking, we can change our lives. So I know we can make aging a positive, vibrant, healthy experience.

I see so much fear among elderly people – fear of change, poverty, illness, senility, loneliness, and most of all, fear of death. I truly believe that all this fear is unnecessary. It is something we have been taught. It has been programmed into us. It is just a habitual thinking pattern, and it can be changed. Negative thinking is prevalent among so many people in their later years, and as a result, they live out their lives in discontent. It is crucial that we always keep in mind that what we think and say becomes our experience. As such, we will pay attention to our thoughts and speaking patterns so that we may shape our lives in accordance with our dreams.

Many of us are now moving into the ranks of elders, and it is time to view life in a different way. We don't have to live our later years the way our parents did. We can create a new way of living. We can change all the rules. When we move forward into our future, knowing and using the treasures within ourselves, then only good lies before us. We can

Louise L. Hay

know and affirm that everything that happens to us is for our highest good and greatest joy, truly believing that we can't go wrong.

Instead of just getting old and giving up and dying, let's make a huge contribution to life. We have the time, we have the knowledge, and we have the wisdom to move out into the world with love and power. We need to change the ways we structure our society, our retirement issues, our insurance, and our health care. We can live long lives that are healthy, loving, wealthy, wise, and joyous. It is time for all of us to be all that we can be during our elder years!

The following letters relate to the issues of aging, and caring for the elderly:

Dear Louise.

I am 90 years old, and I pride myself on the fact that I am in pretty good health. I was very good at playing handball, which I loved doing until about seven or eight months ago, when I was affected very seriously with difficulties in my left leg and my teeth, and with speech problems. I attributed it to the stress and illness that affect old people. I lost my wife five years ago. We were married 63 years. Finally, and most important of all, I have a deeply implanted guilt feeling that I have not divulged to anyone.

I was examined by three doctors and, for 60 days, I went to a rehabilitation center for exercise, but it did not help me. I wanted to know what caused my condition, but none of the doctors were able to tell me.

After reading your book You Can Heal Your Life, *which emphasizes love and joy, I decided I wanted to live to be 100, God willing, and I need your teachings to help me. I feel that if I had the opportunity to attend a class you teach, I would*

22

regain my health in a short time. I am thankful to you for any
recommendations.

Dear One,

I commend you for taking charge of your life and working toward feeling greater joy, peace, and understanding. Losing a spouse of 63 years is a tremendous challenge.

It is important for you to find a sense of purpose in your life, so each day you can look forward to something to validate that purpose. Your purpose might just be to build on your present relationships. Do you have children and grandchildren? What have your interests been in previous years? And, of course, I advocate healing the hurts of the past – let go of any and all resentments and allow love to flow through you. I believe all of us are here to express the love we have always had within.

Many people suffer from guilt and feel an act was so bad, they can never divulge it. However, holding guilt in keeps us from feeling the very love we need, both toward ourselves and others. I encourage you to find someone to talk to about it. It's important that you release your guilt.

Problems with the left side of the body generally represent the feminine, and the right side, the masculine. Because your leg problem is on your left side, I am wondering what feminine figure you may need to forgive or what feminine figure may be involved in a forgiveness you need to bring to yourself. Problems with the teeth often represent indecision. Your speech is your avenue of self-expression. What is it that is so difficult to express? Perhaps it is the very thing you feel guilt about.

I regret to inform you that I am no longer facilitating training programs. My work has taken a new direction, which includes more writing, some lecturing, gardening, and taking care of myself. However, many wonderful teachers are out there who can help you as well as I could.

Check for notices at a nearby metaphysical bookstore or in a local newspaper that gives attention to self-help teachings and teachers.

Know that you are very special and that you are entitled to the many blessings of life. Be very kind and gentle with yourself as you continue your pathway to healing. Affirm: I AM OPEN AND RECEPTIVE TO MY NEXT STEP IN LIFE.

Dear Louise.

I have been working for the past 19 years in the medical profession, and I work with a lot of elders. So many of them are very sad, bitter people. When I greet them with a cheery 'Good morning,' the response I often get is 'Don't get old,' or 'It's hell to get old.'

After many years of hearing this message over and over again, I finally decided to ask one woman, 'What's the alternative?'

She replied, in a very low, gravelly tone, 'Death!'

I try and affirm all good and wonderful things for the patients I see. But I'm feeling stuck. I don't want to hear that message anymore. I want to laugh and dance until my final days on this planet. What can I say to these people? Or better yet, what can I say to myself that will put a stop to this repeated negative message?

Dear One,

A lifetime of eating the 'Standard American Diet,' high in sugar, salt, and fat; using medications for every little ailment; having a negative outlook on life; and believing that getting older means getting sick will produce the elders that you describe. These are people who feel that they are victims of life. In the medical profession, you don't get to see a lot of really healthy older people. It is time for us to totally revamp the way we view our later years. We do not have to live out our lives the way our parents did. It is time to change the rules and the old beliefs. You and I can create a new way of living. We can both laugh and dance until our final days, and so can anyone else who wants to join us.

When people around me are negative, I say to myself, 'It may be true for you, but it is not true for me.' Perhaps it would be more rewarding for you to work in the holistic health field, where you would find those who are actively pursuing health. I would like to see someone create a retirement home that includes a holistic health center. In addition to traditional doctors and nurses, there would be chiropractic, acupuncture, homeopathy, traditional Chinese medicine, nutrition, herbology, massage, yoga, a health club, and so on. This would be a place where everyone could look forward to healthy, carefree later years. I am sure such a place would have a waiting list in no time.

Use the affirmation: I AM SURROUNDED BY HEALTHY, HAPPY PEOPLE. Then watch to see how the Universe manifests that for you.

Dear Louise.

I am a 31-year-old single mother with a 13-year-old daughter. I am planning to enroll in a nursing program. The challenge that I face is that two months ago I became the primary caregiver to my 75-year-old grandmother, who is in the second stages of Alzheimer's.

How do I continue to provide quality loving care under her constant stream of negativity and mentally abusive statements? I love her and am committed to caring for her, but I don't want to lose myself in the process. Also, can you give me advice on how to help my teenage daughter through this? As she told me, 'Granny has already lived her life, but I'm just beginning mine.' Help!

Louise L. Hay

Dear One,
When we are in a state of overwhelm, is it good to stop focusing on the negative. We can never find a good solution when we only see limitations. Take a deep breath. Let your shoulders, face, and scalp relax. Turn the whole situation over to the Universe. Say to yourself repeatedly: ALL IS WELL. EVERYTHING IS WORKING FOR OUR HIGHEST GOOD. OUT OF THIS SITUATION ONLY GOOD WILL COME. WE ARE SAFE!

Then focus on what you could envision as the perfect solution. What is the ideal scene? Put your intentions down on paper. Hold to this vision. Share this with your daughter. Have both of you do constant positive affirmations. Then relax and let the Universe work out how they will manifest. You and your daughter will discover how very powerful you are.

Dear Louise,

I'm having difficulty with the issue of aging. I've become so neurotic about my appearance that I avoid looking in mirrors for days. Then, when I catch a glimpse of myself, I am completely devastated.

Although I have many difficulties at the moment, all of my depression seems to be concentrated on the loss of my youth and beauty. How can I handle this without it interfering with my life?

Dear One,
God has created us as divine, magnificent creatures with rich, full lives to live. We are meant to experience every age, for every age has its own special experiences. From birth to old age, we can live with joy, or we can make ourselves miserable.

Please don't buy into the current social belief that says that youth is the only place to be. If you do, you rob yourself of happiness. Every age is beautiful. Was your youth and beauty so fabulous that you have built no other values in your life? Who taught you that looks are the only things that matter? Do you think that no one will ever love you again? Would you really rather die than get old?

Worrying only helps you age faster. It is unfortunate that the culture and the media place so much emphasis on youth and beauty. While all of us are young at one point, few of us fulfill the current beauty standards. We must stop putting this pressure on ourselves. It is time for you to learn to love the inner child. Keep her happy, and you will look younger each day. Affirm: THE MORE I LOVE MYSELF, THE YOUNGER I LOOK.

Learn to love yourself in the here and now. Do some volunteer work with people who are really in trouble. You have so much to offer them, and it is so needed. Enjoy the rhythm and flow of life.

Dear Louise,

I am having a terrible time believing that God can or will heal so-called genetic or 'old-age' diseases, because it has been ingrained in me from early childhood that certain diseases are 'normal' as you age, and God isn't going to heal them any more than He would heal baldness, weakening eyesight, or gray hair.

I am sure millions of people out there grew up with the same belief, which has been compounded by support from the medical profession. Praying for a healing is difficult when a doctor says, 'It's normal for this to happen as one gets older.'

What do you think?

Louise L. Hay

Dear One,

Just because something is ingrained in you does not make it true. Remember, we once believed the world was flat. What really needs healing is our societal belief that deterioration of our health as we get older is 'normal.' We do not have to believe this. We, as a society, must go beyond our limitations. Your body does not have to wear out; it is constantly renewing itself. (See Deepak Chopra's book *Ageless Body, Timeless Mind*.)

I would find another doctor. You might consider trying a holistic-healing practitioner. Are you aware that the foods you eat could be contributing to your conditions? Shopping at a health-food store and reading some books on nutrition are good ways to increase your knowledge about health and healing.

God gives us exactly what we choose to believe. If we believe in limitation, then we will have it. A good affirmation for you might be: I AM WILLING TO GROW IN UNDERSTANDING, AND I BECOME YOUNGER EVERY DAY.

Dear Louise.

My mother suffers from obsessive-compulsive behavior. She washes her hands at least 100 times a day and repeats thoughts and rhymes over and over. She is now 91 years old and lives with my 98-year-old dad in their home. She is no longer able to take care of the house, but she refuses to let me or anyone else clean the house or help her.

I recently visited her, and she told me not to come around anymore because interruptions to her life make her nervous. I feel very sad that she doesn't want me around, and my heart aches to hold her even though I saw her seven days ago.

I need some insight into dealing with aging parents. How do I let go and respect her wishes?

Dear One,

Please realize that your mother's behavior has nothing to do with you. All behavior and disease is created to fill a need. When we understand the needs our loved ones are trying to meet, it becomes easier to love and support them in their process.

Obsessive-compulsive behavior fills the need to feel in control. The need to control always equals fear. Fear patterns generally start in childhood, because these are the times when we feel the least control over our lives and environment. For many of us, aging is also a time when we feel as vulnerable as we did as children. Remembering how it feels to be vulnerable and afraid can help us provide sensitive love and support to our aging parents.

Help your mother to feel safe as much as she will allow. By first understanding what she wants and what makes her feel safe, you may have more success being with her.

Your mother may choose not to let you in. As heart-breaking as this is, it may become necessary to begin to release the need to feel responsible. Finding support in this process of letting go is very important. You are not alone. Many people are facing the sensitive issue of providing love and support and dignity for their aging parents. Contact Children of Aging Parents, 2761 Trenton Road, Levittown, PA 19056, (800) 227-7294 for information on support and resources in your area.

An excellent book on this subject is *Aging Parents & You*, by Eugenia Anderson-Ellis. Affirm: MY MOTHER AND I MOVE PAST LIMITATIONS INTO FREEDOM. WE ARE FREE TO BECOME ALL THAT WE CAN BE!

Affirmations for
Appreciating the Aging Process

I am young and beautiful – at every age.

I am open to experiencing all that life has to offer.

I contribute to society in fulfilling and productive ways.

I am in charge of my finances, my health, and my future.

I honor and respect the children
and adolescents in my life.

My family is supportive of me,
and I am supportive of them.

I am respected by all with whom I come in contact.

I honor and respect all the elders in my life.

I have all the time in the world.

I have no limitations.

I know that the thoughts in my mind have everything to do with my working conditions, so I consciously choose my thoughts. My thoughts are supportive and positive. I choose prosperity thinking; therefore, I am prosperous. I choose harmonious thoughts; therefore, I work in a harmonious atmosphere. I love getting up in the morning knowing that I have important work to do today. I have challenging work that is deeply fulfilling. My heart glows with pride when I think of the work that I do. I am always employed, always productive. Life is good. And so it is!

Chapter Four

CAREERS

When people ask me about my purpose in life, I tell them that my work is my purpose. It is very sad to know that most people hate their jobs and, even worse, that they don't know what they want to do. Finding your life's purpose, finding work that you love to do, is loving who you are.

Maybe you are in a job now where you feel stuck, or you hate it, or you find that you are just putting in your time to bring home a paycheck. Well, there are definitely things you can do to make positive changes. The most powerful tool you can use to transform your situation is the power of *blessing with love*. No matter where you work or how you feel about the place, bless it with love. I mean that literally. Say, 'I bless my job with love.' But don't stop there. Bless with love the building, the equipment in the building, your desk if you have one, the counter if you work at one, the various machines you may use, the products, the customers, the people you work with, the people you work for, and anything associated with this job. It will work wonders.

If you hate the job you have now, you will take that feeling of hatred with you. Even if you get a good new job, in a short time you will find yourself hating the new one, too. Whatever feelings you have within you now, you will carry to the new place. If you now live in a world of discontent, you will find it everywhere you go. You must change your consciousness now, before you can see positive results in your life. Then, when the new job comes into your life, it will be good, and you will appreciate it and enjoy it.

If you were raised with the belief that you must 'work hard' to earn a living, it is time to let that belief go. Do what you love, and the money will come. Love what you do, and the money will come. You have a right to enjoy earning money. Your responsibility to Life is to participate in enjoyable activities. As you find a way to do something that you enjoy, Life will show you the way to prosperity and abundance. Almost always, that activity is playful and joyful. Our inner guidance never gives us 'shoulds.' The purpose of life is to play. When work becomes play, it is fun and rewarding. Remember: *You* decide what you want your working life to be like. Create positive affirmations to achieve it. Then declare these affirmations often. You *can* have the working life you want!

The following letters relate to the topic of work and career:

Dear Louise.

I recently moved to Atlanta and have started a mail-order business selling vitamins and herbs. I feel good about it and want this enterprise to be a success. Since I am currently working as a temp, and the job will end soon, I am preparing my mail-order business enthusiastically.

I have heard so much about serving the customer and 'doing what I love and then the money follows.' But how can I better serve my prospective customers and not be caught up in 'just making money'? Could you give me some suggestions on how I might do this?

Dear One,

Doesn't it feel wonderful to start your own business! Do you realize that 35 percent of all businesses in America are owned by women, and you are joining their ranks. The sky is the only limit to how far you can take your career. Forget about the money. Have a good product that enhances customers' lives. Give good, dependable service. Go that extra step, and you will have customers for life. Before you open the mail or answer the phone, bless that order or that phone call with love. Pay all your bills on time. Send out your orders promptly. Add a little something extra in each order, perhaps an affirmation card. See all your business dealings as opportunities to bless and prosper each other. When you give with love, then the money comes by itself. Affirm: I DESERVE TO PROSPER. MY INCOME IS CONSTANTLY INCREASING. I AM A SUCCESS, AND I AM SAFE.

Dear Louise.

I am a very capable, intelligent professional man in my 40s (I'm a high school physical education teacher), but I can't seem to hold a job for long. I feel that every time I get into a situation that appears to be ideal, there's some idiot who works above me who thwarts me at every turn. Usually they are jealous of me because I am very popular with the students and can relate to them like a peer. Or, sometimes it's because I tend to speak up when I feel that an important matter needs to be addressed, and the principal or other administrator can't stand to have someone challenge their authority. So, I end up out of a job again.

Do you think I'm the one doing something wrong? Why do I always attract losers into my professional life? Any help would be appreciated.

Dear One,

You are not wrong in any way. However, you are carrying old childhood/family patterns with you into your profes-

35

sional life. Many people do this. Then we don't understand why we have bosses who treat us as one of our parents did. What family member do these 'idiots' who work above you remind you of? I'm not talking about how they look, but how they behave. Who in your family treated you this way? This is the person whom you need to forgive. As long as you carry around the old family baggage, you will always have work problems.

There is no point in merely calling those who work above you 'idiots,' for they are not to blame either. They are only mirroring to you your pattern. They have taken on the role you, on a subconscious level, expect them to play. I suggest you do some mirror work. Sit down in front of a mirror and talk to the parent involved. If, for example, that parent is your father, tell him everything you would find it difficult to say to him in person. When you have let all the frustration and rage out, then tell your father that you forgive him and realize that he was only doing the best he could at the time. From that moment on, whenever he comes to your mind, say: 'I FORGIVE YOU, AND I SET YOU FREE.' Also, every time you think of a former co-worker, say: 'I BLESS YOU WITH LOVE, AND I FORGIVE YOU.' By clearing your consciousness in this way, you will never have these problems on a job again.

Dear Louise.

I am a 26-year-old woman trying to finish up my chiropractic internship, but I feel like a failure because I don't see how I'm ever going to finish school, make a living, and pay off my student loans. Also, I don't even think I want to be a chiropractor! Every time during the course of school that I complained, people would always tell me how much better it would be when I got into a clinic, but now it's even worse.

I am so tired and depressed all the time, and I've gained 50 pounds and have digestive and menstrual problems. I find myself wishing something was seriously wrong with me physically so I'd have an excuse not to finish school. Sometimes I wish I'd have an accident, and I've contemplated suicide. These thoughts scare me, but I feel like what's ahead of me is impossible. My question is: How do I get through this experience that makes me feel like I'm dying? Should I just quit and live with the shame of failure and the huge debts that can't be paid?

Dear One,

Why do you think you would be a failure if you just quit this path that you're on? Who in your family is saying that to you? Whom are you trying to please? It has been my experience that when people do what brings them joy and fulfillment, they are filled with enthusiasm for life. It sounds to me as though you have not found your purpose in life yet. Perhaps being a chiropractor was the fulfillment of someone else whom you were trying to please. What brings you joy? What makes your heart sing?

Go within and trust the process of life to reveal your true purpose to you. You will find that in doing what you truly love, the money will follow, the weight will stabilize, and the digestion problems will subside. In the meantime, find something that really makes you happy, and pursue it. Bless the path you have been on, and know that it was perfect for you at that particular time.

Now it is time to open your arms to the Universe and lovingly embrace yourself as you begin this new unfolding of Divine Order in your life. A wonderful affirmation for you is: I TRUST THE PROCESS OF LIFE. EVERY CHOICE I MAKE IS THE PERFECT CHOICE FOR ME. I AM SAFE; IT'S ONLY CHANGE. I LOVINGLY RELEASE THE PAST, AND I NOW CREATE A NEW AND WONDERFUL CA-

Louise L. Hay

REER THAT IS DEEPLY FULFILLING FOR ME. AND SO IT
IS!

Dear Louise.

*I really do not know what step to take next. I have been an
elementary school teacher, grades 1 to 4, for 29 years. It has
not been an easy career, in that there have been many ups and
downs. At present, I feel like leaving this profession. I am
trying to get a partial disability pension because of stress.
Failing that, I really don't know what to do. I would like to
pursue a career in Mary Kay, because of the loving atmosphere, but I haven't yet proven I can do it, because of all the
demands made on me in teaching. I feel that I no longer wish
to be part of a system that is so unconcerned about the real
problems, such as the dissatisfaction of the children and their
inability to learn in this 'climate.' Changing curriculum is not
the answer. I no longer feel that I can make any difference to
the world of children.*

*I realize that much of what has happened to me in this
lifetime (I am 50, never married, and no children) has
happened so that I could realize that life is really about love
and peace and joy, which I feel most times. But right now, I
need some help in knowing which direction to take, because I
am definitely afraid of what might happen if I am not
successful in my Mary Kay career. I would really like your
suggestion(s).*

Dear One,

It sounds as if you are terrorizing yourself with your own
thoughts. Start to examine what thoughts bring up fear and
what thoughts bring serenity. Until you make peace with
yourself, you will never find it in another job. Stress is an
inside job. If teaching is no longer the right thing for you to

do, then leave it. But leave it with love and joy, not fear. Go for what you really want. Honor yourself and pray for direction. Love yourself. Take the risk and the Universe will support you in ways that you cannot even imagine at this time. You are right; Mary Kay is a great group to work for, and I know you will do very well. Affirm: I MOVE FORWARD IN LIFE TO MY NEXT OPPORTUNITY, AND ALL IS WELL.

Dear Louise,

I have a problem with my boss. I have spent three years trying to discover one good thing about this man. He belittles, patronizes, pits people against each other, and sets us up for failure. One minute he pretends to like you, then he belittles you in front of your peers. Three women have brought discrimination charges against him, and since this is a government setting, he's still here and they're gone.

This guy's not going to beat me, but I believe I'm going to need more help. Any suggestions?

Dear One,

It sounds to me as if you are still trying to win Daddy's love. After reading and rereading your letter, I ask: 'Why are you still working for this man?' I do advocate getting the lessons out of situations we are in, but maybe your lesson is to work on areas of your own life so you do not attract this kind of situation again. Get out! It is not loving yourself to stay in this kind of a situation, and it is not realistic to think you can change this man.

A good affirmation for you might be: I AM A KIND, LOVING PERSON; AND I WORK FOR KIND, LOVING PEOPLE.

Louise L. Hay

Dear Louise.

I am a successful working artist. However, it seems that every once in a while somebody will come by and steal my designs or duplicate my artwork.

This problem is making me resistant to showing my work. I am still very creative, and I still do show all of my work, but the thought invariably crosses my mind: What if somebody steals this design or idea? *Although I have confronted some of these thieves, they seem to care less and have little remorse. There is hardly anything I could do without pursuing it in the court system, a route I don't want to take.*

I would just like to understand why this might be happening. I need an affirmation I can use to transform old, negative energy into something good and also prevent this from happening again.

Dear One,

I feel that your thinking is coming from hoarding and scarcity rather than from abundance. Fearing that someone will steal your work and therefore deprive you of income or recognition is what I call 'poverty thinking.' We always want to know that there is plenty for everyone.

If your work is good, some people will always copy what you do. Think of it as a compliment. Art belongs to the Universe, not to one individual. Share your work freely, and the Universe will see that you are abundantly compensated.

Allow your thinking to become abundant, and your art and work will reflect that state of mind. May you continue to be successful, and may your heart be open and free. Affirm: I FREELY SHARE MY TALENTS AND ABILITIES, AND THE UNIVERSE LAVISHES ITS ABUNDANCE ON ME.

Dear Louise.

I have a problem with my boss. He is a good guy about 90 percent of the time. But for the other 10 percent, he is a ranting, raving lunatic who has horrible temper tantrums that he inflicts upon me (since I'm his secretary). I feel absolutely shattered inside when these episodes occur, and I always feel like quitting my job. However, my personal situation (I'm a single mother with kids) does not allow me to do so.

The strange thing is that after one of his blowups, my boss will be totally calm. I'm always expecting an apology, but one never comes. I'm afraid that if I tell him (during one of his calm periods) that this behavior is unacceptable, he'll blow up at me. What do you think is the best course of action to take?

Dear One,

Your boss was raised in a family where tantrums were normal. He thinks that is the way to behave when things go wrong. It has nothing to do with you. However, you are under the *law of your own consciousness*, and you will always create the world you believe you deserve. This has to be a repeat of stuff that went on when you were a child. You made an excuse then for why you had to endure it, and you are making an excuse now for continuing to endure abuse. It will not be until women build up their own self-worth and self-esteem that they will no longer tolerate such behavior.

I once moved into a building where the landlord was known to frighten all the tenants. I used the affirmation: I ALWAYS HAVE A WONDERFUL RELATIONSHIP WITH MY LANDLORDS. He was always nice to me, and when I moved, he bought all my old furniture. I would suggest you use the affirmation: I LOVE MYSELF, AND I ALWAYS WORK FOR THE MOST WONDERFUL BOSSES. This will become a personal law for you, and no matter where you go, you will find a wonderful boss.

P.S. I run a very successful business. We never mistreat or abuse our employees in any way. We work four-day weeks, and joy and laughter is everywhere. I cannot understand running a business any other way.

Dear Louise.

I'm a 23-year-old actor living in Los Angeles. I'm writing plays and slowly but surely getting small parts in different projects. Lately, though, I feel blocked. I feel as if I've hit a ceiling of my abilities, and I've been there for quite some time. A great part of this problem stems from my resistance to get emotional.

Intellectually, I'm willing to sob or yell or laugh or whatever a part requires, yet in practice, I feel cold and numb, on-screen and off. Do you have any advice to help me break through this ceiling?

Dear One,

I sense a scared little kid within you who is afraid of acting like a fool and being ridiculed. This fear keeps you from having 'fun' with your acting. You can never solve this problem intellectually. Your mind keeps you in control, and that is the only place where you feel safe at the moment.

I believe the Rebirthing Process would be wonderful for you. It is a breathing modality done in a safe, intimate environment that allows you to release the pain and fear of early childhood. There are many Rebirthers around – just begin to ask, and you will find the perfect one.

In the meantime, try using these affirmations to help alleviate your fears and stimulate your creativity: I AM SAFE, AND I AM FREE TO EXPRESS ALL THE JOY WITHIN ME. ACTING IS FUN, AND I LOVE IT!

Dear Louise.

Since the age of four, I have played the piano (by ear), and it's my greatest passion and love. It's all I think about. Each day I ask the Universe to allow me to make a full-time living with music. (Now I do volunteer work at weddings, parties, etc.)

However, two years ago, I went to a pop concert, and since then my hearing has been extremely sensitive. Some tinnitus is there, although the problem is more one of sensitivity. Two doctors have tested me for hearing loss, and there is none. I was fitted for hearing-aid type devices that let in some sounds but block out others that are harmful. Right now I wear earplugs almost everywhere. I have worked in a lot of record stores and gone to many concerts; have I damaged something by being around all that music?

The Universe has given me the gift of being a musician, but now it's being threatened, and I don't understand why. Now it hurts me to hear. What once brought me and others joy, now brings me fear. Will my music be taken from me because hearing it hurts? This would scare almost anyone, but for a musician, it's terrifying. Music is my whole life, and to have it taken away is terrible.

I hope you can help me see some light, because it's getting darker every time I sit before a piano.

Dear One,

It sounds to me as if you have become 'overly sensitive to life.' What past message was so strong that you would destroy the one thing that you love so much? Who would you please if you did not follow your chosen career?

I believe something else happened to you two years ago, and you need first of all to forgive that person or circumstance. Perhaps an old childhood message was triggered. Your hearing sensitivity could be a screen you have put up to keep you from hearing (that is, becoming aware of) an important insight. Take time to quiet yourself and ask your inner wisdom to reveal the message you hear so strongly that you can't hear it at all. Affirm: I LISTEN WITH LOVE AND PEACE TO WHAT LIFE IS TEACHING ME.

Dear Louise.

I've been having difficulty for most of my life when it comes to knowing 'what I want to be when I grow up.' I think it's lovely the way your career unfolded before you, and I admire the work you've chosen.

I'm positive that things will change and shift for me if I just keep working on finding my life's work; however, I often get frustrated with the amount of time my goal is taking. I also feel as if time is running out for me as I get older, even though I'm only 25.

What advice could you share with me as I continue to plot my course to my career summit?

Dear One,

My 'career' did not even begin to unfold before me until I was in my mid-40s. Even then, the start was so small and slow that I did not recognize it. I had no idea that one day I would be doing the work I am doing and on the scale I am doing it. I am what is called a 'late bloomer.'

Perhaps you have much more to learn about life before your work becomes apparent. Today is the only opportunity you will ever have to experience this day. Stay in the now, and rejoice in every moment. Don't let your days slip by in frustration or you will miss out on much of your joy. Take a month of expressing gratitude at every turn. Life loves a grateful person and gives even more to be grateful for. Affirm: MY LIFE IS UNFOLDING IN GLORIOUS WAYS. I AM AT PEACE.

Affirmations for Career Growth

I get along with all my co-workers
in an atmosphere of mutual respect.

I work for people who respect me and pay me well.

My work space is a pleasure to be in.

It is easy for me to find employment.

My income is constantly increasing.

My work is fulfilling and satisfying.

I always have wonderful bosses.

It is a pleasure to come to work.

I have a great work life.

I appreciate my career.

I am at peace with the process of death and grieving. I give myself time and space to go through this natural, normal process of life. I am gentle with myself. I allow myself to work through the grief. I am aware that I can never lose anyone and that I am never lost. In the twinkling of an eye, I will connect with that soul again. Everyone dies. Trees, animals, birds, rivers, and even stars are born and die. And so do I. And all in the perfect time-space sequence.

Chapter Five

DEATH AND GRIEF

A lot of sadness comes to the surface upon the death of a loved one. It's important that you let yourself feel the sadness. Nature has given you feelings to get you through certain experiences and to deny them causes more pain. Remember, death is not failure. Everyone dies – it's part of the process of life.

We all cope with our grief in different ways. There are no rules, so don't make any for yourself. It's okay to get angry and have hysterics. You can't pretend it doesn't hurt, and you need to give your feelings an outlet. Use this time to work on yourself so you can release your negative feelings. You need to get to a point where you feel safe enough to let the old pain come up. If you would allow yourself two or three days of crying, much of the sadness and guilt would disappear. If you need to, find a therapist or a group to help you feel safe enough so that you can release your emotions.

Although grieving takes time, sometimes you feel as if you're in a bottomless pit. Be patient and gentle with yourself. Don't judge yourself for not being with the person or doing enough for the person while he or she was alive. That's just adding guilt to your grief. If your loved one were able, he or she would probably tell you not to worry because all is well.

Sometimes the death of a loved one brings to the surface our own fears about death. We need to understand and work through our own feelings about dying. Since I began working with Aids patients, I have known hundreds of people who have died. Being close to some of these people during the end of their lives has given me an understanding of death that I did not have before. I once thought of death as a frightening experience. Now I know it's just a normal, natural part of life. I like to think of death as 'leaving the planet.'

It's just as important to know what we believe about death as about life. If you have a lot of negative messages within you, then do work to change those beliefs. Meditate, study, read books, and learn to create for yourself a positive, supportive belief in the afterlife. We want to learn to accept death, to allow ourselves to go through the experience it offers with peace and wonder. It is not until we can be at peace with dying that we can really begin living.

The following letters deal with the topics of death and grief:

Dear Louise.

When I was growing up, I had a brother who was ill with a cancerous brain tumor. He died when I was 12; he was 15. He was my only sibling and my best friend. I spent every moment I could with him, fearing he would die if I wasn't by his side. I told him I would never leave him. I still have a lot of guilt, however, that affects me even now as a 24-year-old woman.

In November 1982, my parents, who were with my brother at the hospital, urged me to stay at a neighbor's house so I could celebrate Thanksgiving. I felt that I should go to the hospital, but I didn't because at that stage of my brother's life, he didn't even know who anyone was.

While I was eating Thanksgiving dinner, he died. I feel like I let him down because I wasn't there for him. I feel that if he had felt my love in the room that night, he wouldn't have died. I feel that I disappointed both him and my mom.

Whenever anything negative comes my way, I feel as if I deserve it. Sometimes when I get really angry with myself, I make myself sick. At times, I feel lonely, but I don't talk to anybody, because I know that would make me feel better, and I don't deserve it.

I know I need to overcome this guilt, but I don't know how. Please help me. I want to feel happy inside. I guess I just need to hear that I'm not such an awful person.

Dear One,

Your brother had his own time schedule for leaving the planet. He waited until you were away from the hospital so he could leave peacefully, without you forcing him to stay. What you did was a blessing to him. Most people who die in hospitals do so around 3:00 A.M., when all their relatives are gone.

Was your brother a person who wanted you to suffer? I am sure he would be disappointed to see how you are destroying your life now. Where is the joyous, loving sister he once had? All this pain is only in your mind. I want you, the adult, to forgive the 12-year-old within you and to tell her how much you really love her. Then, I want you to establish a new relationship with your brother. Talk to him, and ask him to help you release this false guilt. Ask for his love and guidance. I know that he wants you to be happy.

Please use this affirmation often: I EXPRESS MY LOVE FOR MY BROTHER BY BEING HAPPY.

Dear Louise.

I'm looking for some clarification regarding an answer you gave in one of your previous Dear Louise columns. You said, 'Animals, like humans, have a time to come and a time to go. And, as with humans, disease is a socially acceptable way to go.'

As a student of 'death,' I think that our beliefs about death and dying affect the way we live and are as important as anything in our search for enlightened living. But did you mean that we choose a disease as opposed to just choosing a time to leave this plane? And if so, do we do that because it's easier for ourselves, or for others, or both? I ask this because it is hard to accept when young to middle-age people just die for no apparent cause.

I would appreciate any light you could shed on this matter for me.

Dear One,

People come to this planet to learn certain lessons, and when the lesson is complete, they move on. The age that they do this is not important. An infant that leaves by crib death could have a more complete life than someone who lived to 97. Soul choices do not make sense to human mind limited thinking.

I believe that when our time to leave comes, we could just go to bed and go in our sleep. But our cultural mind set tells us that we must have 'ways' to die. We use accidents, murders, natural disasters, and, most of all, illness as our vehicles. These are all socially acceptable ways to go. Suicide is not culturally acceptable.

Become a student of 'life,' and as you allow yourself to see a larger and larger picture, you will find that 'death' is only one small, normal, natural part of it. I believe that Life is eternal, and when we leave this plane of action, we move on to new experiences. The more love we learn to give and receive in this life, the more love we will find in our next life.

Dear Louise.

My father committed suicide early this year, and it has been a trying time as I work to heal and move forward from the pain and grief that this has created for me. I find that my spirituality has enabled me to cope with this tragedy much easier than if I had not been exposed to any faith at all.

However, I find myself somewhat confused about my father's soul, and I am interested in what your opinion may be in reference to this matter. One of my relatives practices Buddhism, and she believes my father's soul is not at rest and that he is destined to bear the same pain and agony until he learns his lessons and lives a full life once again through reincarnation. What do you think?

Dear One,

Each person leaves this planet at the right time for him or her and in the right way. I always believe that the particular time and way is a soul choice and that there is never any 'right' or 'wrong' attached to it. I, too, believe in reincarnation and that we come to this planet many times to learn different lessons, and that the circumstances of our births and deaths are different each time. I also believe that we return to be different sexes and different races, to be sometimes rich and sometimes poor. We need to experience it all.

Although many religions believe that suicide is 'bad,' this concept is human mind-created and may not necessarily be the truth. Buddhism has its own belief system. I studied with the Buddhists for a while, and my understanding is that they believe that a soul only stays in the other realm for 49 days and then immediately reincarnates into another life. Having worked with and seen so many people die of Aids, when I see a new baby, I now often say, 'Is that you, Bill? Have you come back to be this precious baby?' Or, 'Is that you, Dave or Michael?' I do see the continuity of life and that every person, place, and thing is energy that is cycled and recycled in the most perfect way.

I honor the challenging time that you have been going

through and know that out of this experience, only good will come. Affirm: I AM SAFE IN THE UNIVERSE, AND ALL OF LIFE LOVES AND SUPPORTS ME.

Dear Louise.

I have just lost the only close friend I had in my life. We had a beautiful relationship that lasted for 28 years. We were always caring and helping one another. He died four months ago, and I still feel lost, lonely, and unhappy without him. I need guidance as to how I can get past this point of grief and make a new life for myself at my age of 48.

Dear One,

I understand how it feels to miss a friend who has left the planet. Grief is a natural and normal process of life. Acknowledge the feelings you're having; they are a wonderful part of you. The intense feelings will pass. It usually takes a full year (you have to go through all the seasons and special days) before you can begin to release them. Know that we are all eternal spirit. Our bodies eventually stop working, but our spirits live on forever.

Remember, we always come into Life in the middle of the movie, and we leave in the middle of the movie. There is no right time to go and no wrong time to go. There is only our time.

Recall with love the close relationship that you enjoyed with your friend, and know that you can form close relationships with others. In the meantime, be kind and gentle with yourself. A good affirmation for you could be: I AM LOVED, AND I AM AT PEACE.

Dear Louise.

I lost my husband a year and a half ago, and I am having a terrible fight learning to live alone for the first time in my life. I can't sleep.

I am a 74-year-old woman, but young and active. My husband worked through his 70th year so we could afford a used motor home to camp and travel with. We made so many plans. Then he became ill and was gone in three months. I have wonderful friends and children who are supportive, but I hate weekends and holidays. I also resent my friends going on trips with their husbands. I get so depressed.

Dear One,

I believe that when a spouse suddenly leaves us, it can be an opportunity to learn more about ourselves. This is not to say having a man in your life would not be appropriate, but rather to use this time now to give yourself the cherished gift of understanding what you are all about and to learn to love, value, and trust yourself at an even deeper level.

You may want to write down what you are feeling at this time. Is it fear? What are you afraid of? Can you learn to look in the mirror and tell yourself that you will always be there for yourself?

On weekends and holidays, do some volunteer work. As you give to others, the pain inside will begin to diminish. At this time of great adjustment in your life, be gentle with yourself. What you are going through is part of the normal grieving process. There are wonderful grief counseling groups that could be very helpful to you. Check in your local phone book.

A good affirmation for you would be: I ALLOW EACH DAY TO SHOW ME THE BEAUTY OF A NEW LIFE. I AM AT PEACE.

Louise L. Hay

Dear Louise.

Recently I learned that my 15-year-old cat had inoperable cancer of the jaw. Within three days, she deteriorated, and yesterday I held her as the vet gave her an injection to end her life. I just didn't know what else I could do at that point. I'm grieving over the death of my pet almost as much as I grieved the death of my close relative about nine months ago.

Please share with me your philosophy about animals in relation to health, healing, and love. What are your thoughts on animal spirit? Do you believe animals can heal themselves? I welcome any insights you choose to give.

Dear One,

Our beloved animal friends creep into our hearts, and when it is time for them to go, we grieve and mourn. In my own life, I have had many animals, and the passing of each one is always a tearful time. This is normal and natural. How kind of you to see that your cat did not suffer needlessly.

Animals, like humans, have a time to come and a time to go. And, as with humans, disease is a socially acceptable way to go. We cannot force a soul to stay. You did everything you could; please do not feel guilt. Release her with love to her next adventure. The next time you allow yourself to get a kitten, it may even be your beloved cat coming back to be with you in a new, healthy body.

Affirm: I RELEASE WITH LOVE, KNOWING THAT LOVE IS ETERNAL, AND WE ARE ALWAYS REUNITED AT THE PERFECT TIME IN THE PERFECT WAY.

Affirmations for Accepting
Death and Overcoming Grief

Death is a door opening to a new life.

I am at peace with the grieving process.

I am at peace with my loved one's passing.

I allow myself the time I need to work through my grief.

Our spirit can never be taken from us,
for it is the part of us that is eternal.

Death is a natural part of life. Everyone
dies within the perfect time-space sequence.

I know that no matter where I am, I am
safe and loved and totally supported by Life.

Our spirit, our soul, is always safe,
always secure, and always alive.

I let the light of my love shine
so that it comforts me and others.

There is no death, only a change of form.

Dis-ease is related to a resistance to the flow of life in some areas, and to the inability to forgive. I forgive myself for not treating my body well in the past. Now I care enough for myself to nourish myself with all the best that Life has to offer. It is my body and my mind, and I am in charge. I help my body, my mind, and my spirit live healthfully by creating a loving atmosphere around myself. I now choose the peaceful, harmonious loving thoughts that create an internal atmosphere of harmony for the cells in my body. I love every part of my body. Life is good, and I enjoy living it!

Chapter Six

DIS-EASE

I believe that we contribute to every so-called dis-ease in our body. The body, as everything else in life, is a mirror of our inner thoughts and beliefs. The body is always talking to us, if we will only take the time to listen. Every cell within our bodies responds to every thought we have and every word we speak.

To permanently eliminate a condition, we must first work to dissolve the mental cause. The symptom is only an outer effect. The mental thought patterns that cause the most dis-ease in the body are criticism, anger, resentment, and guilt. For instance, criticism long indulged in will often lead to diseases such as arthritis. Anger turns into things that infect the body. Resentment that is long held festers and eats away at the self and ultimately can lead to cancer. Guilt always seeks punishment and leads to pain. It is much easier to release these negative thinking patterns from our minds when we are healthy than to try to eliminate them when we are in a state of panic or constant pain. Without reproaching ourselves or feeling guilty, we need to work on how to avoid creating thought patterns of dis-ease in the future.

When we listen with love to our body's messages, we fuel it with the food it needs, exercise it, and love it. It is an act of love to take care of our body. We need to cherish and revere these wonderful temples in which we live. I don't believe that we all have to get sick and wind up in nursing homes – that's not how we're meant to leave this extraordinary planet. I think we can take care of ourselves and be healthy for a long time.

It is time for us to take our power back from the medical

and pharmaceutical industries. We have been buffeted about by high-tech medicine, which is very expensive and often destroys our health. It is time for all of us to learn to control our own bodies and create good health for ourselves, thereby saving millions of lives and billions of dollars. When we really understand the body/mind connection, most of our dis-eases will disappear.

The following letters relate to the topic of dis-ease:

Dear Louise,

My 63-year-old father has just been diagnosed with pros-tate cancer. It's apparently inoperable, and the doctors haven't given him very long to live. My mother is devastated by this. They have made lots of plans for their retirement years, and now it looks as though they're not going to be able to enjoy them together. My father is very depressed and refuses to discuss his illness with us.

I know from reading your books that it is possible to overcome cancer. I'd like to know what I can do to help my father try to fight this illness. And I'd like to help my mother be supportive and strong. Is there anything I can do in this situation? I love my parents very much, and it's terrible to see them this way.

Dear One,

You have given me an opportunity to talk about some-thing that is close to my heart. Prostate cancer, like breast cancer, is preventable and often curable. In fact, most of our dreaded dis-eases come from lifestyle choices – that is, poor nutrition, smoking, using alcohol to excess, drugs, lack of exercise, and a negative mental attitude. There is a very good book out by Larry Clapp called *PROSTATE HEALTH IN 90 DAYS: Without Drugs or Surgery.*

I don't know how advanced your father's case is or how much he has bought into his doctor's opinion, but it is certainly worth looking into. No one has a right to tell us how long we have to live. We accept death sentences when often it is only someone's opinion. Your father needs to realize that this diagnosis is only a wake-up call, and there is much he can do if he is willing to take his health into his own hands. Many people have outlived doctors who told them they would die.

On the other hand, everyone is under the law of their own consciousness and must make their own choices. He will do it his way. You can offer support, but you cannot force. Love your parents enough to allow them to find their own approach to healing. Affirm: I SURROUND MY PARENTS WITH LOVE AND SUPPORT.

Dear Louise,

I am 41 years old, and six weeks ago I was diagnosed with breast cancer. I had a lumpectomy and am now doing chemotherapy. Although I chose the conventional way to treat this illness, I know how important it is to treat my entire body from the inside out.

I've read your books and listened to your tapes, and I understand your beliefs about why disease occurs, but I have some trouble applying it to myself on a daily basis. My mind needs to eliminate the fear of the disease returning so I can spend more time healing. How can I learn to focus more on this? I have repeated your specific affirmations for breast cancer over and over. How do I know if they're working?

Dear One,

Now is the time for you to gather every bit of information you can on alternative/complementary methods of healing

Louise L. Hay

your body, even though you are using the current medical treatments. Expand your knowledge. Learn more about the body/mind connection and the breast cancer/nutrition link. When I had my cancer, I studied everything I could lay my hands on, and it helped to alleviate the fear. I strongly urge you to read *Women's Bodies, Women's Wisdom*, by Christiane Northrup, M.D. It is filled with so much good information for women and how they can gain control over their bodies. I suggest you go immediately to page 303 and read Dr. Northrup's views on breast cancer.

I have learned that most women who have breast cancer are people who put everyone else in their lives first. The breasts represent nourishment, and you are probably a person who nourishes everyone else and have little resources for yourself. Women with breast cancer must learn to say NO! Not 'no' with an excuse, but just plain 'no.' Yes, the people who are used to taking advantage of you will get angry when you first say 'no.' The first 'no' will be the hardest, the second 'no' a bit easier, and by the third time, you will wonder why you didn't do it years earlier. People always take advantage of someone who always says 'yes.' They have respect for people who set boundaries and can say 'no.' This is a big lesson for you. Affirm: I LOVE AND NOURISH MYSELF, AND I AM SAFE.

Dear Louise.

I have had candidiasis for six years. I have had to rely on SSI payments to survive. My family doesn't know or understand the condition. I would not dare tell any friends or people in the community because I am so ashamed.

I still have a lot of stuff to dig up, feel, and release. Can you advise me on how to speed up the process?

Dear One,

I always feel concern when I hear someone say 'dig up' in relation to healing old wounds. Resolving and releasing old issues and feelings is a healing process that requires tender, loving care, and 'digging up' doesn't usually imply this. Sometimes it helps to remember that our inner child is often the one who carries many of our unresolved issues and feelings. As you continue your healing process, remember that tender inner child and provide him or her with an abundance of patience, kindness, and encouragement – as you would any child. You will speed up your recovery process in miraculous ways.

Shame and guilt are your main problems, not your candidiasis. Would you feel 'ashamed' if you broke your ankle or had a cold? Of course not. Guilt comes from a thought that you did something wrong, and shame comes from a thought that something is wrong with you. Neither is true. You are a magnificent, divine expression of life, and you happen to be going through an experience called candidiasis.

Group therapy would probably be very beneficial for you. Knowing you are not alone in this experience can help you overcome negative feelings. I have also found Religious Science churches to be an excellent source of fellowship and support.

Look in your mirror every morning and affirm: I LOVE AND ACCEPT MYSELF, AND EVERYTHING I NEED FOR MY COMPLETE HEALING COMES TO ME NOW.

Dear Louise.
I am a 33-year-old woman who is writing you from Italy. I've read all your books, and I liked them so much that I went to your seminar here. The experience was vital for me!

Thanks to the two-day conference, I was able to get rid of my psoriasis.

Right now, I'm trying to make the right decision about another aspect of my health. I can't decide whether or not to have an operation for hyperthyroidism (as a result of this condition, I also have goiter and palpitations). I have put it off until now because I have been told that after this operation I would need to take medicine every day for the rest of my life, and I'm not sure that I'd be able to do that. In one of your books, you suggested that readers 'overcome their limitations,' and I believe I've done that, but what else can I do to avoid this operation?

Dear One,

All of your dis-eases are different forms of being frustrated in life. I see that your creativity has never been allowed to flourish. For whatever reason, you will not allow yourself to express yourself freely. You did very well in releasing the psoriasis; now, you need to work a little deeper.

I would like to suggest that on a physical level, you work with a nutritionist who does traditional Chinese medicine. On the metaphysical level, there is a Louise Hay-trained teacher in Milan: Max Damioli. Let yourself have a few sessions with him to help you permanently clear out this pattern. When I reach a stuck place in my own life, I turn to a therapist – a well-trained one can often see clearly what is hidden from our own eyes. Affirm: I PARTICIPATE IN MY OWN HEALING PROCESS WITH JOY!

Dear Louise.

I am a 20-year-old female who was diagnosed with HIV a little over a year ago. My husband infected me before we were married. I believe that I am doing very well, as my T-cell count is high, and I am sure that I will be a long-term survivor. I feel this because I was brought up with the influence and knowledge of how positive thinking affects who we are. I have read your books on Aids and on healing your life, and they are very helpful and uplifting.

However, what I want to know is: Do you really think someone can completely cure oneself of HIV or Aids? I am determined to cure myself, but I wonder if it's really possible. If so, how does one go about doing it?

Dear One,

There are people who have cured themselves of Aids – not as many as I would like – but some. It is hard to get statistics because when people heal themselves, they go back into the woodwork because of the stigma attached to HIV/Aids. Niro Assistant, who was written up in *People* magazine and lives on the East Coast, has healed herself and now runs workshops for People With AIDS (PWAs). Caroline Myss was an early worker with PWAs. Her book *AIDS: Passageway to Transformation* (Stillpoint 1987) documents her first case history of a man and his healing. She has also run many workshops for PWAs. Her book, *ANATOMY OF THE SPIRIT: The Seven Stages of Power and Healing* (Harmony Books), is well worth reading by anyone who wants to heal their body, mind, and spirit.

Most people who heal tend to go into an intensive program. They may change their diet; start to exercise; stop smoking and drinking; and use castor oil packs, vitamins, minerals, herbs, therapy, meditation and prayer, and anything else that pertains to their particular case. Therapy is usually necessary to release destructive inner messages, to work on forgiveness, and to create self-love. Most of all, the program must be entered into with joy. So many people enter their healing programs as if they are being punished. Healing is deeper than curing and must come from within.

Affirm: I ATTRACT INTO MY LIFE EVERYTHING I NEED FOR HEALING. Begin to read, and explore your local health food store for ideas and lectures. Love yourself and love your body.

Dear Louise,

I want to thank you for your book You Can Heal Your Life. *I have been practicing many of the things you suggest. For example, I had an ulcer for years, and after understanding the correlation between the disease and the probable emotional cause, I was finally cured, although it was certainly not an overnight process.*

Lately, I have learned that I have 'low blood oxygen at exertion.' Doctors have tried all kinds of tests, but they haven't yet found what's causing this malady. Since I'm a metaphysical student, I believe that things are generated in the mental plane first. Please help me! What's the mental cause for this condition? I would greatly appreciate any advice you may have, as well as any affirmation that is fitting for my particular situation.

Dear One,

I have never heard of this particular illness, and you don't explain much about it. Does this happen when you exercise or walk up the stairs? In any case, let's look at this question from a metaphysical point of view. Blood always signifies joy and family. When there is a blood problem, we are dealing with how the family has either taken away your joy or has somehow prevented you from having joy in your life – at least from your point of view. Oxygen is the breath of life, and healthy blood has the appropriate amount of oxygen.

Our heart represents love, while our blood represents joy. In a healthy individual, our hearts lovingly pump joy throughout our bodies. I envision this joy soaking and soothing and saturating all the cells in your body so that each cell is able to do its best work in an atmosphere of joy. Are you a fun person? Do you laugh a lot? Can you replace fear with joy? How can you allow more joy to be in your life? Is there someone you still need to forgive? Your heart is made for love. Love will heal you. Affirm: I MOVE THROUGH LIFE JOYOUSLY AND FREELY.

Affirmations for Overcoming Dis-ease

I love my body.

My body loves to be healthy.

I appreciate my glorious body.

I listen to my body's messages.

Every cell in my body is loved.

I know how to take care of myself.

I am healthier than I have ever been.

I am in harmony with every part of life.

I lovingly create perfect health for myself.

I give my body what it needs on every
level to bring it to optimum health.

I am constantly increasing my understanding. I am teachable. Every day I open my awareness a little more to the Divine Wisdom within me. I am glad to be alive and so grateful for the good that has come to me. Life, to me, is an education. Every day I open my mind and my heart and discover new insights, new people, new viewpoints, and new ways to understand what's happening around and within me. The more I understand, the more my world expands. My new mental skills are really helping me feel more at ease with all the changes in the incredible school of life here on Planet Earth.

Chapter Seven

EDUCATION

I t doesn't matter what we do in this world. It doesn't
matter if we are bank presidents or dishwashers, house-
wives or sailors. We all have wisdom inside that is connected to Universal Truth. When we are willing to look
within and ask ourselves what we really want and need, and
if we really listen, then we will have the answer. We can't
give our power to other people's pictures of what we need or
of what's right and wrong. We are the authority in our lives.
When we understand that, we can begin to follow the path
that is right for us.

A woman at one of my workshops wanted to be an
actress. Her parents persuaded her to attend law school,
and she was under a lot of pressure from everyone around
her to go into law. However, she stopped going after one
month. She decided to take an acting class because that is
what she always wanted to do. Soon after, she started
having dreams that she was going nowhere in her life,
and she became miserable and depressed. She was having
a problem letting go of her doubts and felt she may have
made the biggest mistake in her life. When I asked her whose
voice she heard in her dreams, she said it was her father's.

There are many people who can relate to this story. The
young woman wanted to act, and her parents wanted her to
be a lawyer. She became confused until she really under-
stood that she had to do what was right for her life. She
needed to connect to her inner wisdom and realize that she
didn't have to please anyone other than herself. She could
love her father and still fulfill herself.

It is one of our challenges to do what is right for us even when those who care about us have other ideas. We are not here to fulfill other people's expectations. I believe that everything does work out for the best in the end, but sometimes it is hard to see that while we are going through a challenging experience. By trusting the Divine Intelligence to help us experience life in the way that is best for us, we empower ourselves to find our own path to fulfillment and to enjoy everything that life has to offer.

The following letters relate to the topic of education:

Dear Louise,

I've always told myself that I'd like to go back to college once my youngest child is in school, but I have four children and a husband, and I'm afraid that he will give me a hard time about it. I feel that he's not supportive enough when it comes to activities with the kids or me. He makes comments such as: 'You wanted all these kids; now you have to make sacrifices.'

But do people have to stop fulfilling their dreams just because they have children? What should I do?

Dear One,

It sounds as if your husband is afraid of losing you if you begin to fulfill your dreams. He fears you may go beyond him. I think he also has strong, traditional ideas of where a woman's place is.

Yet, you have a perfect right to fulfill yourself. No one can think for you unless you allow them to do so. The thoughts you think in your mind are your private thoughts. This is the place where you will begin your changes. Study, read, and listen to tapes. You can find many things in the library.

Create in your mind how you want your life to be. Practice affirmations.

Remember, affirmations are anything and everything you think and say and believe. You want to change your programming of believing that a husband has control over you to one of having a supportive husband. Use these powerful affirmations: MY FAMILY TOTALLY SUPPORTS ME IN FULFILLING MY DREAMS. I DESERVE ALL GOOD IN MY LIFE.

Dear Louise,

I am a college student who has been interested in your teachings for several years. During my vacations from school, I delve into self-help books, work on forgiving and releasing the past, and I try to improve my self-confidence and self-esteem. I attend a challenging university, and my classes, although interesting, are very difficult. During the school year, I end up destroying my mental and physical health by working too hard, overeating, not sleeping, isolating myself from people, and living in a state of constant fear and stress about my grades.

By the end of each semester, I have to 'start over' and rebuild my health and self-esteem again. I plan to be in school for several years, and I do not want to be unhappy during the entire process of my education. Any advice you have would be greatly appreciated.

Dear One,

Why are you giving your 'grades' so much importance? They are only marks on a piece of paper and have nothing to do with your self-worth and self-esteem. Stop doing such a negative number on yourself. I think tests and grades have been blown out of proportion and create so much stress for students. Tests are only to show you how much you do or do not know.

Begin every morning with a few minutes of meditation. Declare your self-worth and self-esteem. Affirm that school gets easier for you all the time. Develop a feeling of gratitude for every experience you have. Learn to find the joy in each moment. It is your life. Love it, and Life will love you in return. Affirm: I AM A SUCCESS IN LIFE. I PROSPER WHEREVER I TURN.

Dear Louise.

I am 19, and I recently failed some important exams and am now spending the year retaking them. I feel upset about this, and I know that if I had worked more diligently, I could have passed and gone off to college. I was lazy and incompetent, and I feel guilty now. God did not put me here to be idle, and I feel like such a sinner. I feel demoralized about the whole thing and would like to make a fresh start. Is there any advice you could give me?

Dear One,

The best fresh start you can make begins with loving yourself. Get off the 'Woe is me!' routine. It is such a waste of time and energy. Regret is a terrible habit and will be with you all of your life if you don't stop it now.

Let's say you learned a valuable lesson and now it is time to move forward. I know this year holds some wonderful experiences for you. I suggest you say this affirmation at least 500 times a day for a month: I LOVE AND APPRECIATE MYSELF. I know your life will change for the better.

Dear Louise,

I am a student in college who is having difficulty with 'communication of energy.' For example, I can't go within to meditate. I also have trouble concentrating at spiritual meetings, music lessons, and art classes. In my view, without this kind of focus, I can't really learn, create, or heal.

One possible cause is that my parents corrected me to be right-handed, although I wanted to use my left hand, so I might have guilt being in the 'right brain' side, which is necessary when you are in the flow. Another possible cause is that I've seen authority figures and partners who are not trustworthy, who tried to control me, and this may have caused a lack of trust to my flow of energy. I also have difficulty with memory and coordination and can hardly sing a song all the way through without interruption. Even if information is logically in my head, it just doesn't seem to come out right. What can I do?

Dear One,

It sounds as if life has become a 'struggle' for you. Life is really meant to be simple and easy. Have you ever considered taking a yoga class? It would help relax your body and open the channels of blocked energy within you.

Forgive your parents for forcing you to be right-handed. They were doing the best they could with the knowledge they had. I feel that you could be perfectly ambidextrous using either hand, as it feels appropriate for different tasks.

It is possible that you have a learning disability, or you might even be dyslexic. These things can be overcome. You might consider taking an educational/psychological test to determine what can help you achieve greater success.

Drop the guilt and the past, the fear and the future. Train yourself to live in the NOW, this moment, today. As you read this, take a deep breath, exhale fully, and affirm: I AM

PERFECT AS I AM. I LEARN EASILY AND EFFORT-
LESSLY. I AM AT PEACE WITH MYSELF. This experience
is only a lesson for you. Re-establish your spiritual connection with the Universe. You are not alone, and you are loved.

Dear Louise.

*I am in the process of designing a program for my junior
high students to help them increase their self-esteem and self-
love. We want to involve those students who appear to be
manifesting the poorest self-images and work with them for
several weeks. I would appreciate any help in the form of
materials and ideas that we could use in developing this
program.*

Dear One,

How exciting that you are devoting your time to working
with our youth in helping them build their self-esteem. This
work is so needed. One of the things I can offer you is my
'Ten Steps to Loving Yourself.' It has been very helpful to
many people. I send you my best wishes in the development
of this program.

Ten Steps to Loving Yourself

1. STOP ALL CRITICISM. Criticism never changes a
   thing. Refuse to criticize yourself. Accept yourself
   exactly as you are. Everybody changes. When you
   criticize yourself, your changes are negative. When
   you approve of yourself, your changes are positive.
2. DON'T SCARE YOURSELF. Stop terrorizing your-

self with your thoughts. It's a dreadful way to live. Find a mental image that gives you pleasure (mine is yellow roses), and immediately switch your scary thought to a pleasure thought.

3. BE GENTLE, KIND, AND PATIENT. Be gentle with yourself. Be patient with yourself as you learn the new way of thinking. Treat yourself as you would someone you really loved.

4. BE KIND TO YOUR MIND. Self-hatred is only hating your own thoughts. Don't hate yourself for having the thoughts. Gently change your thoughts.

5. PRAISE YOURSELF. Criticism breaks down the inner spirit. Praise builds it up. Praise yourself as much as you can. Tell yourself how well you are doing with every little thing.

6. SUPPORT YOURSELF. Find ways to support yourself. Reach out to friends and allow them to help you. It is being strong to ask for help when you need it.

7. BE LOVING TO YOUR NEGATIVES. Acknowledge that you created them to fulfill a need. Now you are finding new, positive ways to fulfill those needs. So lovingly release the old negative patterns.

8. TAKE CARE OF YOUR BODY. Learn about nutrition. What kind of fuel does your body need to have optimum energy and vitality? Learn about exercise. What kind of exercise can you enjoy? Cherish and revere the temple you live in.

9. MIRROR WORK. Look into your eyes often. Express the growing sense of love you have for yourself. Forgive yourself while looking into the mirror. Talk to your parents while looking into the mirror. Forgive them, too. At least once a day say, 'I love you; I really love you.'

Louise L. Hay

10. LOVE YOURSELF . . . DO IT NOW. Don't wait
   until you get well or lose the weight or get the new
   job or the new relationship. Begin now – and do the
   best you can.

76

Affirmations for Achieving Goals

I have a great life.

I stand on my own two feet.

I accept and use my own power.

I explore the many avenues of my being.

I am willing to learn new ways of living.

I feel totally complete and whole.

I accept and use my own power.

I am deeply fulfilled by my life.

I give myself what I need.

It is safe for me to grow.

I love the feeling of freedom when I take off my heavy coat of criticism, fear, guilt, resentment, and shame. I can then forgive myself and others. This sets us all free. I am willing to give up my stuff around old issues. I refuse to live in the past any longer. I forgive myself for having carried those old burdens for so long. I forgive myself for not knowing how to love myself and others. We are all responsible for our own behavior, and what we give out, life will give back to us. So I have no need to punish anyone. We are all under the laws of our own consciousness. I go about my own business of clearing out the unforgiving parts of my mind, and I allow the love to come in. Then, I am healed and whole.

Chapter Eight

EMOTIONAL PROBLEMS

E motional problems are among the most painful of all. Occasionally we may feel angry, sad, lonely, guilty, anxious, or frightened. When these feelings take over and become predominant, our lives can become an emotional battleground. Many of us feel so flawed that we believe we are not good enough and never will be. And if we find something wrong with ourselves, then we are going to find something wrong with others as well. One of our biggest problems is that most of us haven't the faintest idea of what it is we need to let go of. We know what isn't working and we know what we want in our lives, but we can't see what is holding us back.

We need to think for a minute about our patterns and problems. What categories do they fall into – criticism, fear, guilt, or resentment? Do they fall mostly into one area or into a combination of areas? Is it fear that always comes up, or guilt? Are you very, very critical or resentful? Let me point out that resentment is anger that is stuffed down. So if you believe you are not allowed to express your anger, then you have stored a lot of resentment.

We cannot deny our feelings. We cannot conveniently ignore them. Chronic patterns of self-hate, guilt, and self-criticism raise the body's stress levels and weaken the immune system. So it is our task to remove the reasons for these feelings so that we can become healthy, whole individuals. Everything in our lives is a mirror of who we are. When something is happening out there that is not comfortable, we have an opportunity to look inside and say,

'How am I contributing to this experience? What is it within me that believes I deserve this?

Then, we need to realize that it doesn't matter what anybody else did to us or what we were taught in the past. Today is a new day. We are now in charge. Now is the moment in which we can create the future for ourselves. We definitely can, because we have a Higher Power within that can help us break free from these patterns if we will allow it to happen.

The following letters deal with the topic of emotional problems:

Dear Louise,

I have been fighting severe depression since my marriage broke up five years ago. I did have a loving relationship with my husband for nearly 11 years, but he abused drugs and alcohol, was a compulsive spender, drove us into bankruptcy, and had an affair with a close friend. I've had two relationships since then, both of which turned out very badly. My last relationship nearly drove me to suicide.

I'm sure my basic problem is my relationship with God, which I thought was pretty good until my world fell apart. Within three months of the breakup, I lost everything: my husband, my home, my credit rating, my career, and my emotional health. I've been a student of metaphysics for years, so my first thought was: How can this be happening to me? I pray; I meditate; I affirm; I tithe; I'm a kind and loving person.

I want so much to express and receive love, to enjoy the wonders that life has to offer, and to feel close to God. But it's very frustrating to see my friends enjoying all the things that I would love to enjoy: loving mates, sexual relations, family, home, prosperity, and purpose in their lives. I feel like everyone around me has discovered the secret to life, while I'm still stumbling and struggling. When I look back, it seems that everything and everyone I've ever loved has been taken from me.

When I read these words, I cringe because I sound like such a whiner and a victim, but it's just that the hopelessness and despair are so overwhelming. Can you help me?

Dear Louise,

The reason you are in so much despair is that you are missing the whole point of your problem. No wonder it all seems so helpless. You have been marinated in self-pity for years. Dry your tears and let's go to work. When we are children, we learn what love is like by what we experience in our home. Was love expressed in your home as soft and tender? Was it yelling and screaming and doors slamming? Was one of your parents an alcoholic? Did your parents adore each other? Were they faithful, or was there infidelity? We learn how to have relationships by watching our parents. When we grow up, we tend to re-create these same relationships. It sounds to me as if you are re-creating either your father or your mother in all your relationships. Probably your bosses, too. You will continue to do this until you release this pattern *within you.*

You need to work on forgiving your parents and releasing them. You will do this best in some sort of therapy group. Look for something through your church, or read the local New Age papers. If you are serious about changing your pattern, Life will bring you the next step. Take it! Stay away from relationships for a bit and learn to love yourself. When you love who you are, then you will attract someone who can love you. Affirm: I FORGIVE MY PARENTS, AND I AM FREE TO LOVE MYSELF.

Louise L. Hay

Dear Louise.

I became very dependent on my analyst. In my mind, she was the mother I never had. I trusted her, and I did not want to make her angry or disappointed. When difficulties appeared and she let me down, I felt deserted, unloved, and worthless again. I contacted several different analysts and a few therapists.

I am currently working with your audio tapes, especially Anger Releasing. *While I do this work, many different feelings come up – a lot of anger, sorrow, and despair. Afterwards, I feel calm and relaxed for a few hours, but I don't feel as if anything is being accomplished. What else can I do?*

Dear One,

I think the first thing you need to understand is your dependency on others to make everything all right for you. No one can do this. If they make you believe they can, then of course you will feel abandoned and angry when they do not deliver.

It sounds to me as though you have been proving to yourself that no one can help you. Running from one therapist to another without really working on yourself is useless.

Know that you are a powerful being and that you have the wisdom and knowledge within you to heal yourself. Work toward getting more in touch with the divine wisdom and love within you so you can take charge of your life and create a peaceful, healthy, loving and prosperous life for yourself.

Some affirmations for you could be: I HAVE THE CAPACITY TO MAKE DECISIONS FOR MYSELF. I ACCEPT MY FULL POWER. I AM ALWAYS SAFE. I TRUST THAT LIFE IS HERE FOR ME.

Dear Louise.

I am writing to you because I am at the end of my rope. I have been recovering from anorexia nervosa for almost nine years (I'm 24). I've been in and out of hospitals and on and off the therapist's couch, so to speak, and I am totally frustrated with the entire psychotherapy profession — and with myself as well. I have spent the past several years reading a lot about changing belief systems, but to little avail. I've tried doing affirmations and have read several of your books, and I just can't seem to remove this all-pervasive sense of worthlessness that's been with me as long as I can remember — I do not exaggerate here.

I'm tired of spending money I barely have on books and tapes that do not help. Most of all, I am tired of beating myself up for everything I think, say, and do. I've had major depression in the past, and I find myself falling back into that abyss again (and my weight is extremely low). What am I missing, Louise? What is wrong with me that I can't grasp this idea of changing beliefs/changing reality on a gut level (I understand it intellectually, of course)? Can you recommend any techniques, tapes, or exercises I can try? I'm on the verge of giving up on everything and everyone.

Dear One,

What a powerful woman you are. You are more powerful than therapists, doctors, hospital personnel, and even books and tapes. No one can force you to heal yourself. You are far too powerful. One of these days you may want to turn this powerful energy toward your healing process instead of toward the destruction of your body.

There is not anyone in this world who can beat you up as well as you can, and you are very good at it. Now the big question is: 'What is so horrible about you that you need to punish yourself in this severe way?' I have asked this question to thousands of people, and no one has *ever* given

Louise L. Hay

me an answer that made sense. As difficult as your problem has become, you are still only dealing with self-hatred. And self-hatred is only hating thoughts you have about yourself. Thoughts can be changed.

You know, my dear, ALL OF LIFE IS THINKING! No matter what you are doing or not doing, you are thinking. Your thoughts shape your life! This is why it is so important that we all learn to take control of our thinking. We are just beginning to learn the significance of this concept. Thinking is a natural law. Our thoughts create our experiences. What we think about is what we get. You have allowed your thinking to get out of control and run rampant in ruts of self-hatred.

Without knowing all the details of your personal history, I do know that somewhere in your childhood, someone told you that you were worthless. Or perhaps they treated you in a way that made you assume you were 'no good.' These were opinions that came from an ignorant person who also had a lot of self-hatred. Being the good little girl that you were, you believed them and have acted on that premise ever since.

Because you are a free person, you have the freedom to continue their pattern of abusing you, or you can decide that it is time to live in another way. Each of us comes to this planet to learn to love ourselves in spite of what 'they may say or do.' You are an old soul and have come in with a more difficult lesson. Being an old soul, you also have many more resources on your side to help you. You have the potential to be a powerful healer. Every good healer I know has been through many dark nights of the soul.

So I do have a suggestion for you. You have had the therapy, and you have read the books and listened to the tapes. You know all that. Now, go and volunteer in an Aids ward or a children's hospital. Get out of yourself long enough to help others. You will be amazed at what a miracle this will create in your own life. It will contribute enormously to your healing experience. It will also bring much love into your life.

Dear Louise.
I am a 23-year-old woman who has experienced two serious cases of depression in the past. For several weeks now, I have been experiencing extreme sadness, but it's not like either of my previous depression periods in terms of the pain. I don't even know what the sadness is about. I feel as if I am experiencing the depression again, but a different part of me feels okay, and the other part feels very sad.
Depression runs in my family, but it has a different effect on each of us. I don't want this illness anymore, but I don't know where to begin or how I need to change my thoughts.

Dear One,
Let me share what I believe about depression, or anything else that seems to run in the family. I feel that we copy our behavior from other members of the family, usually a parent, which in turn manifests the same pattern for the 'hereditary' dis-ease. When we change our belief system, we can change the pattern.

Depression represents anger you feel you do not have a right to have – hopelessness. You say you had been feeling sadness for a period of time. However, I want you to think back to when you were a small child. Did you feel sadness then? Were you pretty much a loner? Do you have the tendency to hold your feelings inside instead of expressing them? We often go through life covering up our feelings in different ways as we grow older. We find many distractions to keep from experiencing those unwanted feelings.

Please find someone to talk with about your sadness, perhaps a counselor or a support group. It sounds as if there are a lot of bottled-up feelings inside you. When you release them, you will release your pain. A good affirmation to repeat to yourself could be: I LOVE AND CHERISH MYSELF. Please say it at least 500 times a day.

Dear Louise.

I have realized for a long time that anger and resentment can play havoc with my body, but up until now I have had no way to stop. I am destroying myself, and I don't know where to turn.

I work six nights a week and am trying to keep a relationship going, but it's hard because he works days. We get along fine in many ways, but we have a lot of problems because we don't see each other. I have an eating problem, a spending problem, resentment, anger, and self-hatred. I am frustrated and don't know who to turn to.

I feel that nothing is worth the effort anymore, and I will never get out of this vicious circle. Please give me some advice on what to do.

Dear One,

Your letter tells me that you feel it is time to take charge of your life. The point of power is always in the present moment, and we can begin to make changes right here and right now. Thoughts can be changed and so can self-destructive patterns. Those that have been with us for a long time take work. I think it would be beneficial for you to be in some sort of support system. Check in the front of your phone book under 'Community Services' for the appropriate group. I also think it would be good for you to do daily mirror work and reassure yourself: I TURN WITHIN AND FIND ALL THE COMFORT AND WISDOM THAT I NEED.

Remember, you are the most important person in your

life. Until we begin to value ourselves enough to meet our own needs, we cannot expect others around us to do it. Take it one step at a time.

Dear Louise.

I want to thank you for assisting me in my healing. You played the very important role of putting me on the right track for releasing a six-year depression.

I still have a way to go since I have a lot of reprogramming of my manic side to do. Could you explain how manic depression can be faced? What lessons must I do to get a handle on my manic self?

Dear One,

When you talk about manic depression, you are talking about an imbalance of energy. Somehow you decided that you did not have the right to be yourself. What happened six years ago to make you flee from life? On one level you were squashing your energy for fear that you had no right to express your feelings, especially anger and depression. On the other level, in order to compensate, your pendulum has been swinging wildly and completely overshooting reality, thus becoming manic. In both cases, there is a denial of reality and a great desire to 'go home,' to be at home spiritually.

You need to learn that you have the right to exist as you are. There is no one to run from and no one to please. You are a divine expression of life, and you came here to express yourself in all your magnificence.

Affirm: I AM AT HOME IN THE UNIVERSE, AND ALL OF LIFE LOVES AND SUPPORTS ME. This is true of you on the deepest level of your being, and your inner child needs to know and accept this.

Louise L. Hay

While my books and tapes can be of much help to you, I am assuming that you are working with a professional counselor. If you don't know where to go, call the National Self-Help Clearinghouse at (800) 952–2075. There is always help available.

Affirmations for Emotional Health

I now live in limitless love, light,
and joy. All is well in my world.

I claim my own power, and
I lovingly create my own reality.

My level of understanding is constantly growing.

I am beautiful and everybody loves me.

I am in the process of positive change.

I love and approve of myself.

I trust Life, and I am safe.

I accept my uniqueness.

It's safe to look within.

Life supports me.

I envelop my entire family in a circle of love – those who are living and those who are dead. I affirm wonderful, harmonious experiences that are meaningful for all of us. I feel so blessed to be part of the timeless web of unconditional love that brings us all together. Ancestors who lived before me did the best they could with the knowledge and understanding they had, and children not yet born will face new challenges and will do the best they can with the knowledge and understanding they will have. Each day I see my task more clearly, which is simply to let go of old family limitations and awaken to Divine Harmony.

Chapter Nine

FAMILY RELATIONSHIPS

W e all have family patterns, and it is very easy for us to blame our parents, our childhood, or our environment for the present condition of our lives. If we grew up in a family where criticism was the norm, then we are going to be critical as adults. If we grew up in a family where we were not allowed to express anger, then we are probably terrified of anger and confrontation, and we swallow it and let it reside in our body. If we were raised in a family where everybody was manipulated by guilt, then we are probably going to be the same way as adults. We probably run around saying 'I'm sorry' all the time, and can never ask for anything outright. We feel we have to be manipulative in some way in order to get what we want.

As we grow up, we begin to live these false ideas and lose touch with our inner wisdom. We need to realize that we can go beyond our family's limitations. We are the ones who suffer when we hold on to past grievances. We give the situations and the people in our lives power over us, and these same situations and people keep us mentally enslaved. They continue to control us when we stay stuck in 'unforgiveness.' We need to let go of the beliefs that hurt us. This allows us to be free from the needless cycle of pain, anger, and recrimination that keeps us imprisoned in our own suffering and prevents us from creating positive, affirming relationships with ourselves and others.

If we want to be accepted as we are, we have to be willing to accept others as they are. We always want to have our parents accept us totally, and yet often we are not willing to accept them as they are. Acceptance is giving ourselves and others the ability to just be. It is arrogant to set standards for others. We can only set standards for ourselves. And even then, we want them to be more like guidelines than standards. The more we can practice self-acceptance, the easier it is to drop habits that no longer serve us. It is easy for us to grow and change in an atmosphere of love. We must strive to love others, to forgive their past behaviors, and in order to do this, we must first learn to love and forgive ourselves.

The following letters relate to the topic of family relationships:

Dear Louise.
My problem is my domineering, controlling mother. I acknowledge the fact that she has had a lot of problems (she contracted polio when I was only 5, and a year later my father left to marry another woman), but I feel utterly suffocated when I am with her. I have told her that I appreciate the fact that she has always given me and her other children 100 percent, and I know that she did the best she could under difficult conditions, but I have also told her that she cannot 'have' my life. I am now living my life for me.

It has taken me many years to break away from my mother's control, and also other controlling people, such as my ex-husband. Louise, how can I be close to her now? She is nearing 80 years old, and her years are beginning to show. I really want to be close, but I feel that I need to stand about ten feet away from her and close an open door when I visit her home. Thank you for your advice.

Dear One,
When older people complain about their children pulling

away, they forget that they are the ones who initiated the situation. Parents who say to their children, 'Don't say that, don't do that, don't think that' are cutting off communication. Also, parents who smother and control and try to keep this up long after the child is an adult also put up barriers to a loving relationship.

You are not responsible for your mother's choices in life. You are responsible for *your* choices. Having a dominating parent almost ensures having a dominating spouse. Bravo for you for moving away from both of them. You may never be able to be close to her, and IT IS NOT YOUR FAULT. Drop the guilt.

I know you want your mother to accept you exactly as you are without trying to change you. Now, give her the same space. Accept her exactly as she is. If she is like most dominating people, she repeats herself over and over. Write down the things she says often, and number them. Then when she goes into the routine that bothers you, you can say to yourself, 'Oh, there goes #7.' Or, 'She is combining #6 with #4 this time.' It will help you to see things in a new perspective and not always react as though you were five years old.

Affirm: I HAVE A JOYFUL, LOVING RELATIONSHIP WITH MY MOTHER. Do this affirmation daily for six months and see what happens.

Dear Louise,

I am a mother-in-law trying awfully hard to get along with my daughter-in-law. My grandson is dying of a disease that is incurable. I understand that my daughter-in-law and my son are going through an awful time – as I am, too. I love them dearly.

My daughter-in-law wants me to show my love physically. She says I don't care and thinks I'm awful. I just don't know

what to do. I can't show my love like that because it isn't how
I was raised. What is wrong with me? Why am I so ashamed
to show my love to my children? When they were young, I used
to kiss and hug them, but now that they're grown up, I feel
ashamed. I just don't know what to do. Please help me. This is
making me sick.

Dear One,

First of all, please realize that nothing is 'wrong' with you.
You are a divine creation of the Universe and infinitely
worthy of giving and receiving love.

From your letter, I perceive you as someone who is more
comfortable saying 'I love you' than hugging and kissing. As
you indicated, this is partly due to the messages you received as a child. Most likely, physical touching was not
encouraged in your home. Children have a high need for
physical contact and reassurance. If these needs are not met,
they can interpret this lack of physical contact as meaning
something is 'wrong' with them. As that idea becomes a
belief about themselves, they develop a sense of shame
about their bodies and physical needs. To keep themselves
safe and not expose their supposed 'flaws,' they cut themselves off from physical contact with others. But this belief
that you are 'wrong' or 'flawed' does not have to be true for
you anymore. (A wonderful book that describes the process
of healing this type of shame is *Healing the Shame That Binds
You*, by John Bradshaw.)

Something else for you and your daughter-in-law to
consider is that we all experience love in different ways –
some of us need to be hugged and touched; others need to
hear the words 'I love you'; still others need to see a material
demonstration of love, such as flowers or candy. We sometimes get into trouble with our loved ones when they prefer
to experience love in a different way than we are most
comfortable demonstrating love. By taking the time to

understand our loved ones' preferences and by sharing our own, we can better communicate the love we feel for one another.

Finally, I believe your daughter-in-law may be finding fault with you at this time due to her own feelings of fear and inadequacy. Bless her and remain compassionate without taking on her projections. Affirm: I AM FILLED WITH AN ABUNDANCE OF LOVE, AND I EXPRESS THIS LOVE FREELY. EXPRESSING LOVE IS SAFE FOR ME.

Dear Louise,

I am a 35-year-old woman who has lived away from my parents for seven years now. I find that when I go home, I almost always revert to a child who is unable to take care of herself. When I am with my parents, I can't imagine how I can pay my rent, go to work every day, etc. It creates a fear of returning to my current home, making me question my abilities and self-worth.

Of course, when I do come home, it is no problem to pick up my responsibilities and continue on with my life as always. The problem is that I find myself dreading visiting my childhood home, which troubles me because my parents are getting on in years, and I want to be able to spend as much time with them as I can. Any words of wisdom that may ease my anxiety about 'going home'?

Dear One,

What you are really asking me is: 'How can I grow up?' Having lived with your parents for so long, there is a part of you that probably still enjoys being treated as a child and being taken care of. When you go to your childhood home for a visit now, you may feel that strong pull once again to have the carefree life of a little girl.

95

However, you were strong enough to leave home after 28 years of comfortable security, and you created a life of work and responsibility for yourself. I know you are now strong enough to reprogram your mind when you visit your parents' home. Instead of fear and anxiety about losing your independence, change those thoughts into love for your aging parents. A good affirmation for you could be: I AM NOW A COMPLETE, SECURE, INDEPENDENT ADULT, FULLY CAPABLE OF TAKING CARE OF MYSELF AND SHARING MY LOVE AND STRENGTH WITH MY PARENTS.

Dear Louise.

My sister and I live in different parts of the country, but we have always kept in touch. Whenever I've had problems, I've always felt that I could call my sister and talk to her about them. She's single, has a good job, and plenty of money. I'm divorced and have four teenagers that I've raised by myself. I've been having a lot of trouble with my oldest son lately, and it helps when I can call my sister and discuss things with her.

Recently, when I've called and begun talking about my son, my sister has interrupted me, saying she doesn't want to hear about it. She has told me that she is tired of my negative attitude about teenagers in general and my son in particular. She asked me not to call her again until I had changed my attitude.

I'm very hurt by this, and I don't know what to do. I want to have a good relationship with my sister, but she just doesn't understand what it's like to raise a teenager. Is there anything I can do to correct this situation?

Dear One,

Why don't you make sure the next time you talk to your

sister you speak only of pleasant things. Tell your sister how much you love and appreciate her. Then, if you must talk about your children, talk about all the things you love about them. I think your sister is tired of being a dumping ground for your problems. Instead of being hurt, use this as an opportunity to heal your family situation.

How often do you tell your oldest son how much you love him? Do you thank him or praise him for the good things he does, or does he just get to hear what he is doing wrong? I know you have a lot of work cut out for you, raising four teenagers, and there are times you want to pull out your hair. However, we often forget how difficult it is for the teenagers to go from being children to adults. They need praise and love more than ever at this time. I am sure you could turn your son around by loving him and letting him know that you understand his difficulties. Affirm: MY ELDEST SON IS A JOY AND A BLESSING, AND I LOVE HIM.

Dear Louise.

I am a 38-year-old woman from a very dysfunctional family, where emotional and physical abuse has been passed down from my grandparents to my parents to myself and other siblings. After years of work on myself, I have overcome the depression, job losses, and physical ailments that used to overwhelm me.

The problem is that now that I am healthier, I have a hard time dealing with my family and all the oppressive junk they dump on me. No amount of positive talk has ever worked with them, and they try to suck me dry. In essence, I do not feel love for them, but only a physical attachment because they are blood relatives. Sometimes I have wished them dead so that I could end this pattern that they so strongly try to pull me down with. Am I okay for feeling this way? How can I continue feeling positive when they're always weighing me down with bad news and negativity?

Dear One,

When you were a child, you were forced to take the abuse that your family dished out. Now you are 38 years old, and you have done a great deal of work on yourself – why are you continuing to take their abuse? You are not here to change them. You are here to heal yourself and to love yourself. They do not have to die in order for you to be free. You can walk away right now. Have compassion for them. Do not continue to play their sick games. It is not an act of love for you to continually subject yourself to negativity.

You do not live your life the way *they* want you to, and they do not live their lives the way *you* want them to. It is as simple as that. Go your separate ways. You are on your own spiritual healing pathway. Increase your own understanding by studying and by letting go of the past. Bless your family with love, and let them be. Affirm: I RELEASE MY FAMILY WITH LOVE, AND I AM FREE TO EXPERIENCE HAPPINESS THAT IS MEANINGFUL TO ME.

Dear Louise,

My sister is obese and has many related health problems (her weight-induced diabetes requires her to be on dialysis twice a week). Even though she is not supposed to eat sugar, she periodically goes on eating binges and neglects to take her insulin. She has a wonderful husband and small child, and I don't understand why she seems to be committing a slow suicide. What can I do or say to help her?

Dear One,

I know it is hard to love someone and see her living in a way that you believe is not good for her. But each of us is on our own particular pathway of life, and none of us really has a right to judge anyone else. We each have our own lessons to learn, and you don't know what your sister's lesson is. It is said, however, 'When the student is ready (and, I believe, not a moment before), the teacher will appear.' Surely, that will happen to her.

So love her and let her be. Affirm: EACH MEMBER OF MY FAMILY, INCLUDING MY SISTER, IS HAPPY, HEALTHY, WHOLE, AND COMPLETE. EVERYTHING IS WELL IN OUR WORLD. This affirmation, worded to suit our own particular situation, is one we all might use for our families. Then we can trust that every experience is really for our highest good.

Dear Louise,

I am having a difficult time working through jealous and angry feelings stemming from uneven distribution of parental attention, love, and material things. My parents have always been generous to three of my brothers and sisters, but withhold from the 'middle' three – even now that we are adults. I do not believe that my parents' behavior will change, and the obvious inequities have caused great tension in my family.

I yearn to be free of jealousy and anger and feelings of unworthiness, and I dream of a healing in my family that will allow strong, loving relationships to develop.

Where do I go from here?

Dear One,

You only waste time looking for healing in your family. This may never happen. You are not responsible for anyone else's attitude or behavior. The only one you can heal is you and your own inner pain. It is not what has happened; it is how you are choosing to respond to it.

If you could believe that you chose to come into your family for a reason, then what do you think is the lesson you are supposed to learn from this experience? I believe we choose families to learn specific lessons and to rise above them. Your feelings of jealousy, anger, and unworthiness only harm you. Will you forgive them? Will you learn to love yourself and create a good life for yourself? These are the spiritual challenges that we all go through. Drop the right and wrong issue. You cannot change what was. Your only power is in the present moment. Whenever you think of your parents, bless them with love. Begin to look for all the good you did get from your family. Develop strong, loving relationships elsewhere. You can always create the ideal family among your friends. Start each day with gratitude by affirming: I AM DIVINELY BLESSED, AND I LOVE MYSELF AND LIFE. Today is your day for happiness.

Affirmations for
Rising Above Family Patterns

I bless my family with love.

I allow others to be themselves.

I make my own decisions.

All my relationships are enveloped in a circle of love.

I have the power to make changes.

I release all old hurts and forgive myself.

I let go of old family limitations
and awaken to Divine Harmony.

All my relationships are harmonious.

I have compassion for my parents' childhood.

I release all criticism.

At any moment I have the opportunity of choosing love or fear. In moments of fear, I remember the sun. It is always shining even though clouds may obscure it for a while. Like the sun, the One Infinite Power is eternally shining its light upon me, even though clouds of negative thinking may temporarily obscure it. I choose to remember the Light. I feel secure in the Light. And when the fears come, I choose to see them as passing clouds in the sky, and I let them go on their way. I am not my fears. It is safe for me to live without guarding and defending myself all the time. When I feel afraid, I open my heart and let the love dissolve the fear.

Chapter Ten

FEARS AND PHOBIAS

Y ou could say fear is rampant on the planet. You can see and hear about it in the news every day in the form of wars, murders, and greed. Fear is a lack of trust in ourselves. Because of that, we don't trust Life. We don't trust that we are being taken care of on a higher level, so we feel we must control everything from the physical level. Obviously, we are going to feel fear because we can't control everything in our lives.

Trust is what we learn when we want to overcome our fears. It's called taking the leap of faith. Trust in the Power within that is connected to the Universal Intelligence. Remember, the power that supplies your breath is the same power that created the Universe. You are one with all of Life. The more you love yourself and trust Life, the more Life is here to love you, support you, and guide you. You can trust in that which is invisible, instead of trusting only in the physical, material world. I'm not saying that we do nothing, yet if we have trust, we can go through life much easier. We need to trust that we are being taken care of, even though we're physically not in control of everything that is happening around us. Read Matthew 6.

Fear is a limitation of our minds. People have so much fear about getting sick or about becoming homeless or whatever. Anger is fear that becomes a defense mechanism. It protects us, yet it would be so much more powerful to stop re-creating fearful situations in our minds and love ourselves through the fear. We are at the center of everything that happens in our lives. Every experience, every relationship, is the mirror of a mental pattern that we have inside us.

Love is the opposite of fear. The more we are willing to love and trust who we are, the more we attract those qualities to ourselves. When we are on a streak of really being frightened or upset or worried or not liking ourselves, isn't it amazing how everything goes wrong in our lives? It is the same when we really love ourselves. Everything starts to go on a winning streak, and we get the 'green lights' and the 'parking places.' We get up in the morning, and the day flows beautifully.

We need to love ourselves so that we can take care of ourselves. We have to do everything we can to strengthen our hearts, our bodies, and our minds. We must turn to the Power within, find a good spiritual connection, and really work on maintaining it.

The following letters relate to fear and phobias:

Dear Louise,

I am a married man in my early 30s, and my wife and I have two young children. I have a recurring fear that one might consider irrational, and I wonder if you can help me overcome it. Basically, I am constantly afraid that my wife will die and leave me alone. Every time she drives off in her car, I fear that she will have a car accident. I'm even afraid that she'll fall in the bathtub or have some other freak accident in the house.

I know that it is silly to worry about such things, but I can't seem to get these feelings out of my mind. My wife is young and vital, and there is no real reason for me to think that she won't live for many more decades. But my mind isn't co-operating with my logic. Can you help?

Dear One,

What was your greatest fear when you were a child? What I am hearing in your letter is the voice of a little child who had to deal with abandonment very early in life. Did someone in your family die and leave you? Perhaps there was a divorce. When was the earliest time you can remember having these feelings? Your feelings are not irrational at all; they come from a time of loss in your childhood. It is a good thing you are reaching out for help.

Now that you have found happiness with your wife and children, you fear that it will be taken from you. Some sort of counseling or grief therapy would be very good for you. You are blessed to have the Lifestream Center in Roanoke. Go and talk to the people there. I would suggest Carolyn Bratton. You will find them very helpful in releasing your fears. A good affirmation for you would be: I DESERVE ALL GOOD IN LIFE, AND I AM SAFE.

Dear Louise,

Thank you for your book You Can Heal Your Life. *You hit so many things right on the head for me that I just sat and cried after I finished reading it. You have helped me identify some problem areas that I can improve upon!*

I have a question about compulsive behavior. I find myself checking the alarm clock ten times every night to make sure the alarm is on. I am super-organized in my life, and I am always having to touch things a certain number of times or ways in order to feel 'even.'

I have seen this condition discussed on talk shows, but of course no cause was discussed, and the only cure suggested was the inevitable medicine. It's becoming quite an obstacle for me. I was hoping you could shed some light on this subject for me.

Louise L. Hay

Dear One,

I am hearing the voice of a child who feels so unsafe. Perhaps when you were young you were never allowed to make a mistake, or you were punished severely when you did. Or maybe you were a child that invented rituals in order to survive a dysfunctional part of your life. What were the 'rules' in your childhood?

It would help you immensely to make a list of all the rules you learned as a child and who said them. This may take you several days to complete while you remember them all. Go over this list one by one and ask yourself, 'Is this the rule I still want to follow today?'

As a child, you had to obey the rules of your family, but now you are grown up and can make your own guidelines as they apply to your life today. Remember, rules can change just as we do. What was an appropriate rule for you as a child may not be an appropriate rule for you as an adult. Give yourself permission to breathe and grow. Allow yourself to make mistakes and learn.

I AM FREE TO BE ME is a good affirmation for you. Say this to yourself constantly throughout the day for at least a month. Your healing pathway has begun.

Dear Louise,

I am a 27-year-old woman who has had a very hard life. I've had family problems, financial disasters, and problems with my boyfriend of three years. I've been under so much stress that I have developed anxiety, panic attacks, stomach trouble, and I cannot breathe at times. Sometimes I think I'm going to suffocate. I also have psoriasis, and I've tried everything for it, but it just won't leave. I believe in holistic medicine and mental healing, but I'm still sick and scared of getting worse. I want to get well and have a beautiful, loving, healthy life.

What should I do? What do you suggest? Why is this happening to me? I feel so 'out of control.' Please help.

Dear One,

You have focused on stress and fear for far too long. For the next week, I want you to carry a timer with you. Set it for every half hour. When it rings, take three very deep, slow breaths, and silently say to yourself, 'All is well, all is well, all is well.' Begin to bless your health with love. Life has given you enough breath to last as long as you shall live. As you slow down, you will begin to trust life, and I'm sure your psoriasis will disappear. Our skin protects our *individuality*, and you feel so threatened in life. A yoga class would be beneficial to your mind and body. Many YWCAs offer yoga at a nominal fee.

The door to your heart and to your dreams opens inward. This means that you must learn to relax before you can solve your many problems. I know you feel that if only you could solve your problems, you could relax, but it doesn't work that way. In order to take the pressure off, you need to make space in your heart for other possibilities to happen.

Please join a 12-step program. They don't cost any money, and you need to find yourself in a group of people you can trust who are working to solve their problems. Affirm: I LEAVE MY PAST BEHIND. I TRUST LIFE. I AM SAFE.

Dear Louise,

When I was little, I was fiercely afraid of the unknown, especially the idea of Satan, ghosts, aliens, etc. I still experience this sensation of fear, and I'd like to now assure my inner child that she is safe. After years of Catholic school, I got used to calling on Jesus for help when I felt scared. But I no longer want to rely on other entities of power for my sense of safety in the world. I want to know that I can provide this for myself. I notice that I feel small in my mind in comparison with grandiose beings such as Jesus and Satan, so it feels funny to imagine myself as equally powerful. I think this Catholic business has been confusing to me as I've grown up. I would like advice on seeing myself as safe from the occult. Can you help me in this area?

Dear One,

It is so sad that people use fear to control others. I can see that you had a fear-dominated childhood. So did I. No person, place, or thing can have any power over you unless you allow it. You are allowing 'memories' of false beings to dominate your thoughts. I suggest that you visualize cords going out from your solar plexus and lower abdomen to these ideas of ghosts, aliens, and Satan. Affirm to yourself, out loud: I KNOW I AM DIVINELY PROTECTED AT ALL TIMES. I NOW CALL BACK MY SPIRIT FROM THESE FALSE ENTITIES, AND I AM SAFE. Then, imagine yourself pulling back these cords and pulling your power back. Do this daily, as often as you need to, until you have a strong feeling of power within you.

This is one of your spiritual challenges – TO BRING YOUR POWER BACK FROM 'IMAGES' OF THE OCCULT. Satan is NOT a 'grandiose being.' Satan is an idea in the minds of humans that is used to dominate others. Separate superstition from the truth of your being. You are safe.

Dear Louise,

Last year my apartment was broken into twice, and now I have trouble being in the house alone at night. It is hard for me to sleep, despite prayers and affirmations.

Last night, I forced myself to go into my room and close the door. I prayed and asked God why I was afraid and strange thoughts came to me that implied I had been molested by my stepfather. Because of all the emphasis lately in the media regarding childhood incest, I don't know if I was molested or if I'm just imagining it. There is an eight-year period of my life that I have little or no memory of, but I don't want to create something that isn't there.

I don't know what to do or where to go from here. I just know that I am tired of feeling as if my heart will pound out of my chest every time I hear a small noise.

Dear One,

You do not need to suffer anymore, nor do you have to do this alone. Go see a practitioner immediately or find some therapy. You need to work with someone who has clear vision and can guide you carefully through this period. At least attend an Al-Anon meeting where you will find loving fellowship and understanding wisdom. Many people have been helped through many different crises by attending Al-Anon.

No matter what the outer circumstances, the only thing you are really working on is loving yourself. And loving yourself is loving God. You are God's loving creation, and you deserve the best in life.

Know that you are on your healing pathway and affirm: I AM NOW ATTRACTING WHATEVER HELP I NEED TO SOLVE THIS ISSUE AND TO LOVE MYSELF EVEN MORE.

Dear Louise,

I feel that I must write and tell you how much I've learned from your books. When I was 15, I was sexually abused by my brother. Harboring resentment for him has caused me great mental anguish. At 27, I started to have anxiety attacks, and

109

that developed into agoraphobia. I went to a doctor for about two years, and I thought I was cured, yet I find that I'm still scared at times.

After reading your books and going into therapy, I'm beginning to see the light at the end of the tunnel. Maybe I'm expecting things to happen too fast. I do love myself, but maybe not as much as I would like. If you could offer any advice, I would appreciate it very much.

Dear One,

Agoraphobia usually has to do with extreme self-hatred and fear of not trusting yourself. Self-hatred is only hating a 'thought' you have about yourself. Thoughts can be changed. Every thought we think and every word we speak goes out from us and comes back to us as experience. Self-hatred or self-dislike can only come back to us as negative experiences.

Remember, to love yourself is to heal yourself. The door to the heart opens inward. It is impossible to love ourselves until we have forgiven. This does not mean to condone others' poor behavior, but to free ourselves from our prison of bitterness and resentment. When you have truly forgiven, love will come easily. You need to love yourself much more. There are many aspects of your life that will heal when you do so. A good affirmation for you would be: I TRUST MYSELF, AND I TRUST LIFE TO SUPPORT AND PROTECT ME. I AM SAFE, AND ALL IS WELL.

Dear Louise,

I grew up in a household where there were many fights and where I was often afraid for my life. I was always being told that I was crazy and that I didn't know what I was talking about. I've grown up being afraid that I really am crazy, and as a result, I tend to just do 'sane' things. I feel like I'm not truly living.

As I've progressed, though, I'm beginning to see where my fears originated. However, I'm still afraid to be free for fear that I will be considered 'crazy.' Can you give me an affirmation to help me heal from my childhood trauma? I can't stand being a 'good girl' anymore. I feel like I'm in prison.

Dear One,

You need to separate the lies that you were told about yourself as a child from the truth of your being. Your parents had been deeply traumatized as children, and they grew up believing many false ideas about life. This is why they created the atmosphere of your childhood. Frightened people lash out without knowing what they are saying. So, begin to believe that all the negative things they told you about yourself are NOT TRUE! As a child, you did not know this, but now you are an adult, and you can reason with adult thinking.

It is the child within you who is frightened. So now is the time for you to take your inner child under your loving wing. When it is too frightened, say to it, 'THE PAST IS OVER. I AM HERE NOW TO LOVE AND PROTECT YOU. NO ONE WILL EVER HARM YOU AGAIN. YOU ARE BRIGHT AND BEAUTIFUL. YOU ARE LOVED, AND YOU ARE FREE.' Repeat this over and over to your inner child until she begins to relax and trust you.

Do go to a few Al-Anon meetings. You will learn a great deal about how to heal your family traumas. As you heal yourself, you will also begin to have compassion for the pain your parents lived with.

Affirmations for Releasing Fears

I am willing to release my fears.

I live and move in a safe and secure world.

I free myself from all destructive fears and doubts.

I accept myself and create peace in my mind and heart.

I rise above thoughts that attempt
to make me angry or afraid.

I release the past with ease and trust the process of life.

I am willing to release the need for this protection.

I am now willing to see only my magnificence.

I have the power to make changes.

I am always divinely protected.

Each of us is part of a harmonious whole. I know there is a Divine blending of energies as I work and live joyfully with my friends. We support and encourage each other in ways that are fulfilling and productive. I have wonderful, harmonious relationships with everyone, and there is mutual respect and caring on both sides. I can live with dignity and peace and joy. I am healthy, happy, loving, joyful, respectful, supportive, productive, and at peace with myself and my friends.

Chapter Eleven

FRIENDSHIP

Friendships can be our most enduring and important relationships. We can live without lovers or spouses. We can live without our primary families, but most of us cannot live happily without friends. I believe that we choose our parents before we are born into this planet, but we choose our friends on a more conscious level.

Friends can be an extension or a substitute for the nuclear family. There is a great need in most of us to share life experiences with others. Not only do we learn more about others when we engage in friendship, but we can also learn more about ourselves.

Relationships are mirrors of ourselves. What we attract always mirrors either qualities we have or beliefs we have about relationships. The things we don't like about our friends are either reflections of what we do or what we believe. We could not attract such people if the way they are didn't somehow complement our own lives. When the bond between friends becomes strained, we can look to the negative messages of childhood to understand why. For instance, if we have a friend who is undependable and lets us down, we need to turn within. We need to see where we are undependable and when we let others down. Then, we need to perform a mental housecleaning, removing the negative messages and learning to accept ourselves so that we can accept others.

It's pointless to run around trying to heal all of our friends. We cannot force others to change. We can offer them a positive mental atmosphere where they have the possibility to change if they wish, but we cannot do it for or to other people. Each person is here to work out his or her own lessons, and if we fix it for them, then they will just go and do it again, because they have not worked out what they needed to do for themselves. All we can do is love them and allow them to be who they are.

The following letters explore the topic of friendship:

Dear Louise,

I am a nice-looking woman in my late 20s who has befriended a woman in my apartment building who doesn't have many friends. She is overweight, not physically attractive, and has very low self-esteem, but I find her very intelligent and funny. Although I enjoy her company most of the time, she tends to put me down a lot. She'll say things such as: 'Oh, look at that pimple on your chin.' 'Why is your hair so dry?' 'You have really fat calves,' etc.

I never respond in a negative fashion because I guess I feel sorry for her, but her comments are really starting to get to me. I guess she feels that since she is not attractive, she has a right to pick other people apart. I don't want to hurt her feelings, but I'm afraid I'm just going to blow up one of these days and let her have it.

What can I do to resolve this situation without having to sever this friendship?

Dear One,

I don't think you have to blow up. Just call her on it. She probably does not know what she is doing. We are often unaware of the things we say and do because they are such habits. Next time she criticizes you, just say to her, 'That was a very critical remark,' or 'You really criticize me a lot; are

116

you aware of it?' Once you have said it the first time, you have the opening to remind her as she does it again. 'You are being critical again.'

Or you can make a game out of it. Tell her: 'Every time you criticize me, I am going to say Purple Pumpkin.' You can do this in a loving way. If she chooses to feel hurt, then that is her problem. Feeling sorry for her lets her get away with unloving behavior. No wonder she has few friends. If you really like her, let her know what she is doing. Then, she has the option of changing or not. Affirm: I AM ALWAYS OPEN AND HONEST IN A LOVING WAY.

Dear Louise,

I have a close friend, who is my only friend, and we have had a platonic relationship for about 30 years (he is 70; I am 54). At times, though, I feel that he has a bad influence on my health and spirituality. It seems that he actually saps my life energy, leaving me depleted, ill, and depressed (he has suffered from depression for years). He does not knowingly have this effect on me – he is kind, generous, and caring. But for about ten years, I have had this gnawing impression of a dark, negative side to him that pulls me away from the Path of Light and onto a path of darkness.

About 20 years ago, we were told by an astrologer that we had a karmic Saturn bond. I feel that this relationship is a painful dilemma, and I am at my wit's end to know what to do. Any response you could give me would be deeply appreciated.

Dear One,

There are many people who are 'drainers.' They unknowingly sap the energy of those around them. Depression is anger turned inward. People who are depressed have great

Louise L. Hay

anger over situations that they feel powerless to change. They do not speak up. Perhaps your friend is still angry over something that happened in childhood. His depression is not your depression unless you choose to take it on.

Now why would your 'only friend' be a person who drains you? Is this what you deserve? Don't build your life on a remark made by an astrologer 20 years ago. Even if true, you can learn your lesson and let go. Don't be at your wit's end. Move on. You are a young woman. You have a whole life ahead of you. There are millions of people in Chicago, and it is time for you to get out there and bring some fun, cheerful, loving people into your life. Go for the joy, and turn your whole life around. Repeat often: I AM OPEN AND RECEPTIVE TO A NEW LIFE.

Dear Louise,

I am a woman who lives with my best friend of ten and a half years. As I have grown and become more self-loving and have raised my self-esteem (after overcoming a dysfunctional childhood), my best friend/roommate has become more and more co-dependent. She's extremely jealous and threatened by any relationships I have with people, especially my intimate relationships with men.

Every time I begin to date or grow close to a man, she suddenly has some kind of stress attack, or she'll create some kind of 'accident' or emergency. Last year out of the blue, she announced that she was bisexual and that I was the object of her obsession. She started acting weird — eating my food, crossing boundaries she had never crossed before.

I have considered moving out, but I have hung on for financial reasons. I value this friendship, but all this has left me feeling very confused. How can I handle this situation amicably? Please help.

118

Dear One,

Your friend is terrified of losing you. Yet she is not ready to do personal growth work of her own, so the gap between you is widening. You may have to choose between your own growth and self-worth and what remains of a friendship that you seem to have outgrown.

NEVER, NEVER hold on to a poor situation because you 'want' something from someone, especially for financial reasons. It is a strong message to the Universe that you do not trust life to take care of you. And you will always be sorry.

Keep working on your own self-worth and self-esteem. Come from the space of 'what is best for me?' You have done too much work on yourself to allow someone else to tear this down. Affirm: OUT OF THIS SITUATION ONLY GOOD WILL COME, AND WE ARE SAFE.

Dear Louise,

I am at a loss as to what to do with an old friend of mine. She seems to pull away every time we start to get close. We've been friends for 19 years, and I still feel that I have to be the one who keeps the friendship going. For a while, she'll be open and loving, and then she'll pull this aloof, distant act that I find very confusing. We have talked about this problem throughout the years, and she says that if she acts like this, it is not intentional. She says she considers me one of her best friends, but then I'll send her a funny fax at work, and she won't respond for weeks.

It's hard to explain, Louise, but I have always had this psychic ability to know if she is in trouble, and I feel a strong bond with her. What do I do with someone who is so afraid to need someone else?

Louise L. Hay

Dear One,

I hear your concern about your friend, and I am glad to know that you have a psychic link with her so you can respond when you feel she is 'in trouble,' as you say. That part is wonderful; however, the whole thing about friends is that we accept them as they are, not as we wish they would be. Remember, she accepts you as you are in spite of the fact that you have been trying to change her for 19 years.

Enjoy the friendship you have with her, when you have it. I have a different relationship with each one of my friends, and I let them all be as they are. I have many friends whom I love dearly, yet we may only see each other once or twice a year or maybe once every two years. I rejoice in the time I have with them and think of them fondly when I do not see them.

So, love and accept her as she is. See her when you can. Make peace with yourself with respect to this particular relationship. Affirm: I ACCEPT MY FRIENDS AS THEY ARE, AND THEY LOVE AND ACCEPT ME IN THEIR OWN WAYS. ALL IS WELL IN MY WORLD.

Dear Louise,

I have an ethical dilemma. I have two friends (a male and a female) who are up for the same promotion at work. This new job requires the applicant to have a four-year college degree. Although both of my friends' résumés state that they have graduated, I happen to know that this isn't actually the case and that my male friend only completed one year at a junior college. I'm so afraid that he will be the one to get the job and that my other friend will lose out.

I don't know what to do. Should I keep my mouth shut and let the Universe take care of things? Should I tell my male friend that I think he's wrong to pursue this job? Is it any of my business? I don't know.

Dear One,

We all spend so much time observing what other people are doing and wanting to set things 'right.' However, each of us is under the law of our own consciousness and will be treated accordingly. Therefore, we do not need to interfere in things that are none of our business. Unless there is danger to other people involved, I do not believe in meddling. Every time I have done that it has always backfired on me.

Unless this promotion interferes with your own position, I would leave it alone. Don't make this *your* issue. Use the affirmation: THE PERSON WHO IS PERFECT FOR THIS JOB RECEIVES THE PROMOTION. Then watch how the Universe decides to handle the situation. Visualize harmony and professionalism in the office, with each person doing his or her work in an atmosphere of respect and joy. Know that you are all safe and protected.

Dear Louise,

I am a 40-year-old man who is a partner in a business with a friend of mine. About three months ago, my partner hired his sister, a very unattractive, overweight woman with a mustache, to work at the front desk of our business. She had just been fired from another position and has a husband and child to support, so my friend felt sorry for her, as did I. Unfortunately, this situation isn't working out. This woman is abusive to clients, customers, and other employees. She is inefficient in her job, and frankly, her lack of concern over her appearance turns people off.

I believe that the negative energy this woman is emanating is hurting our business and making everyone unhappy, but I don't want my partner to be put in an awkward position by my insisting he fire his own sister. Also, I feel guilty about suggesting that this woman be put out of a job again. I am in a quandary. Any advice?

121

Louise L. Hay

Dear One,

You allow this woman to abuse your clients and your other employees, and yet you're afraid of hurting HER feelings! Why would you want to do this? Do you really want to destroy your business and your employees' morale? Why are you punishing your good employees? You must put a stop to this instantly, or you won't have a business. The good of the whole group is always more important than the good of one person, especially if that person is a troublemaker.

Having said that, now let's realize that this is the time for you to test your diplomatic and assertiveness skills. You can practice by writing down what you want to say beforehand and even giving it a trial in front of a mirror. You need to have a very honest professional talk with your partner. You need to get the message across to him that he is not helping his sister in the long run by allowing her to continue this inappropriate behavior. Perhaps you can get your partner to see that he will help his sister better her life if he informs her gently, but truthfully, that she needs to change her behavior. His sister could use some form of therapy from a professional counselor to explore the reasons for her excessive weight and abusiveness. She is probably covering up her pain. She needs real change from within. Please stop enabling her to continue on this destructive pathway. Affirm: I HAVE A HARMONIOUS, PROSPEROUS BUSINESS. EVERYONE IS SAFE.

Affirmations for
Strengthening Friendships

I am willing to release the pattern
in me that attracts troubled friendships.

I love and accept myself, and I am a magnet for friends.

All my friendships are successful.
I am a loving and nurturing friend.

I trust myself, I trust life, and I trust my friends.

Loving others is easy when I love and accept myself.

Even if I make a mistake, my friends help me through.

I deserve to be supported.

My friends are loving and supportive.

My friends and I have total freedom to be ourselves.

My love and acceptance of
others creates lasting friendships.

I believe that each lifetime before we are born we choose our country, our color, our sexuality, and the perfect set of parents to match the patterns we have chosen to work on in this lifetime. Each lifetime I seem to choose a different sexuality. Sometimes I am a man, sometimes I am a woman. Sometimes I am heterosexual, sometimes I am homosexual. Each form of sexuality has its own areas of fulfillment and challenges. Sometimes society approves of my sexuality, and sometimes it does not. Yet at all times, I am me – perfect, whole, and complete. My soul has no sexuality. It is only my personality that has sexuality. I love and cherish every part of my body. I am at peace with my sexuality.

Chapter Twelve

GAY AND LESBIAN ISSUES

The gay and lesbian communities have the same problems everybody else has, plus much of society pointing their fingers at them and saying, 'Bad!' Often their own mothers and fathers are also saying, 'You're bad.' This is a heavy load to carry, and it's difficult to love yourself under these circumstances. It is not surprising that gay men were among the first to experience Aids.

No matter what your sexual orientation is, it is perfect for you. When we are referring to relationships, it applies to all of us, no matter if your relationship is heterosexual or homosexual. Even science is now recognizing that sexual orientation is something that we are born with and not something that we choose. If you are heterosexual, imagine what it would feel like if you were told you had to become a lesbian or a gay man. We must not put ourselves or anyone else down for something as simple and natural as sexuality.

I am not trying to create guilt for anyone. However, we need to look at the things that need to be changed in order for all of our lives to function with love and joy and respect. Fifty years ago, almost all gay men were closeted. Now they have been able to create pockets in society where they can at least be relatively open. And many of you may be unaware that in Victorian days, the prevalence of separate worlds (in business, politics, parenting, etc.) for men and women made male-female relations so strained that women commonly turned to other women for their most intimate relationships. Romantic friendships were also common among young middle-class men. No one considered such relationships a sign of homosexuality. In fact, the term wasn't even invented until the late 19th century.

The point is that love is where we find it. Fashions in love change from country to country and century to century. We have certain so-called norms at the moment, but they, too, will change in time. Let's drop the judgments and rejoice in love when we see it. This is a time for healing, for making whole, not for condemnation. We must rise out of the limitations of the past. We are all divine, magnificent expressions of life.

The following letters explore some gay and lesbian issues:

Dear Louise,

A dear friend and I have reached an impasse over the subject of homosexuality. She assumes that it would be impossible to be on a spiritual path and be homosexual, because once one is enlightened, homosexuality would be gone. I, on the other hand, disagree.

We live in a very provincial area where people are generally very conservative. Neither of us even knows any homosexuals. Since you have done a great ministry with Aids patients, what are your thoughts? Please help me understand.

Dear One,

I am glad to share my views with you and your friend. Your willingness to go beyond your fears is a step of great spiritual growth.

What we do not understand, we fear. It is so easy to put someone else down in order to make ourselves better, bigger, more important, or even holier. There was a time when we shunned lepers, the retarded, and people of color. Now, most of us have gone beyond those limited beliefs.

How can we call ourselves spiritual beings when we see any form of life as 'less than'? What pride and arrogance we have taught ourselves. And how it keeps us from our own divinity. When will we stop teaching our children to hate any person, place, or thing?

Hatred is learned. Any hatred or prejudice you have was learned. Babies are not born hating anyone. As we grow spiritually, we drop old, limiting ideas about ourselves, others, and life.

You say you don't know any gay people, and yet at least 10 percent of the population is gay. You do know some, and they could be anyone in your world: co-workers, students, children, relatives, parishioners, or neighbors. However, they may be afraid to let you know who they really are for fear of your condemnation.

We always seem to resist change because we fear it. Think of all the changes that were previously resisted in our history, and how much better off we are because of them. At one time, it was thought that integrating African Americans into the army would bring down morale. And it was not long ago that women were fighting for the right to vote! These things seem silly now, but at the time, they were extremely sensitive issues reflecting much fear and misunderstanding.

Homosexuals are not wrong. They are just being who they are. God did not make a single creature who is wrong. A person with skin of another color is not wrong. You and I are not wrong. We are all God's perfect children.

I know many people will be offended by my stand on this issue. Resistance is often the first step toward change. Didn't you first resist your spiritual growth? For years, I have been a champion of unpopular causes, for I truly see all human beings as worthy and needing love and acceptance.

Every one of us has a soul, and our soul has no sexuality. When we leave the planet, the only thing we take with us is our capacity to love. Let us all grow and open our hearts to include everyone. Affirm: I OPEN MY HEART TO LOVING UNDERSTANDING OF ALL OF LIFE.

Bless you for wanting to expand your own horizons of understanding.

Dear Louise,

In the last five years, I found out that I have a sex chromosome disorder called Klinefelter's Syndrome. It means that I have more female sex chromosomes and more genes. I am about to start taking female hormones and hope within a year to get my body completed as a female, because I know I am female below the skin.

I feel like a female trapped in this male body, and the only way out is to have this operation. I don't want to be this way the rest of my life. I want to look as feminine on the outside as I feel inside. I dress every day as a female when I go to church, bank, shop, pay bills, go to dinner, etc. I am a female as my friends know me, but I am not really who I should be – a true lady in my physical body. I know you are not a doctor, but some insight would help a lot from a real lady.

Dear One,

We do come into this life with such interesting challenges, and we all need to make peace with whatever they are. It sounds as though you are at war with your body. If you really feel you are a female inside, then you need to create great self-esteem for yourself as a woman. Many women have masculine-looking bodies. You are merely one step beyond. Just love who you are, as you are. You are going in the right direction. Remember, no operation will give you the inner peace you seek. This inner peace can only come from loving yourself.

Actor Christopher Reeve has said that the most important thing he learned from his paralyzing accident is that 'he is not his body.' Beyond the personality, beyond the physical body, is the soul – the soul you have always been and always will be. Connect with yourself on the soul level, and you will be at peace.

Dear Louise,

As a clinical social worker, I have the responsibility for co-facilitating a drop-in support group for men with Aids. I have long believed in the value of meditation and creative visualization; however, the men within our group consistently reject any use of relaxation exercises, tapes, creative visualizations, or meditation. While I believe they have the right to do so, I am also frustrated by this decision and see it as a passive acceptance of their illness. Our groups too often descend into the 'ain't it awful' scenario – which I feel only perpetuates issues of weakness or loss of control. How have you solved this problem?

Dear One,

I understand how frustrating it can be to want to help people who don't seem able to get the message. One of the things we have to understand is that we cannot force anyone. All we can do is what we do, and they either accept it or reject it as they wish. I often say, 'I am not a healer, and I am not your mother. I just give out information, and you are all grown up and can make your own decisions.'

We must not let our ego get in the way. If you are like me,

you still have plenty of work to do with those who are willing to listen. Keep doing what you are doing, because it is greatly needed.

Dear Louise,

I have been living with HIV for many years, and I'm doing great. I am strong and healthy. However, the religion I was raised in is very much against my lifestyle. They often call me 'evil' and 'satanic.' I try to ignore these attacks, but they really hurt. They also hurt my family members, who are still in this church, but who are choosing to love and accept me anyway.

Louise, how can I deal with my deep hurt and resentment? I have forgiven many times, but the expressions of hatred seem to be continual. I am a gentle, loving, compassionate man. I know that God loves me and answers my prayers. How can I dissolve my bitterness so that it won't damage my health?

Dear One,

I can empathize with your hurt and confusion surrounding who you really are. But remember, when we are children, we have no say about the religion we are brought up in. Perhaps your parents are still using the religious choices of their parents and grandparents. As a loving, conscious adult, I doubt that you would choose a religion that belittles any of God's precious creatures. You need to separate what you were taught as a child from what is the truth of your being. As a divine, magnificent creation of the Universe, you are abundantly loved. Choose another religion. I encourage you to experience a new attitude to spirituality by attending a Science of Mind or Unity church.

It is up to you to open up to all the love and approval

around you. You begin this by loving yourself unconditionally. You are not responsible for the unenlightened remarks being made by members of this particular church. You are responsible if you choose to listen to them and to believe them. If I called you a 'Purple Pig,' you would laugh and pay no attention, no matter how many times I repeated it. Who are you giving your power to? Stick with the people who love and accept you as you are. A good affirmation for you is: AS A MAGNIFICENT CREATION OF A LOVING GOD, I AM INFINITELY LOVED, AND I ACCEPT THIS LOVE NOW.

Dear Louise,

I am a 35-year-old woman who is living in a wonderful home with a male roommate. We are both gay. I think the world of him, and since I've been attending the Science of Mind church in my area, I've begun to feel that I can love anyone I choose – man or woman. My challenge is this: I love my roommate, who is a very good-looking guy. We were friends before we lived together. Now I fear telling him about these feelings because not only would it 'floor' him, but I am sure it would cause feelings of discomfort. I need to get a handle on this. Please help.

Dear One,

One of Life's givens is that not everybody we love will love us back. Accept that, and don't ruin the good friendship that you have. Of course, you can love anyone you choose, and it is enriching to love as many people as you can; however, since your roommate is gay, you need to consider how you can express your love to him in a way that will not cause him discomfort.

You may not be in a satisfactory relationship of your own

131

right now, and you may be confusing your need for a complete relationship (love and sex) with your feelings for your roommate. By focusing on someone you can't have, you are closing the door to allowing the perfect person to enter your life. Too much denial is going on here.

Affirm: I HAVE THE PERFECT, LOVING MATE, AND SO DOES MY ROOMMATE. WE SUPPORT EACH OTHER'S CHOICES.

Dear Louise,

I am a gay man in my late 20s who has had a series of tumultuous relationships with my boyfriends. It seems that every time I get involved with someone, this person tries to get me to change. He will expect me to stop drinking, stop partying, stop going out with my friends, and just spend all my time with him alone. Frankly, I don't want to change. I enjoy my social life and don't want to give it up. Unfortunately, my boyfriends don't believe that I'm being faithful to them (I am), because I go out a lot. This problem has caused the end of some close relationships, and I don't know what to do about it. Why should I have to change my life for someone else?

Dear One,

You ask a lot from your boyfriends. I wonder if you give them the same freedom that you demand. Of course you don't have to change, but don't expect others to be close to you if you remain the social butterfly flitting around. Do you like them to flit around with you, or do you just want them to sit home and wait for you?

Maybe you are too young emotionally to settle down in one relationship. Do what you do until you don't have to do it anymore. At some point in your life, partying will get really dull, and you will look for more fulfilling things. But for now, have your fun, and do an affirmation that says: I BRING INTO MY LIFE THE PERFECT MATE WHO AC-CEPTS ME EXACTLY AS I AM.

Affirmations for Embracing Sexuality

It is safe for me to explore my sexuality.

I express my desires with joy and freedom.

God created and approves of my sexuality.

I love myself and my sexuality.

I am safe and secure in my love for myself.

I give myself permission to enjoy my body.

I go beyond limiting beliefs and accept myself totally.

I am safe to be me in all situations.

My sexuality is a wonderful gift.

I am worth loving.

Good health is my divine right. I am open and receptive to all the healing energies in the universe. I know that every cell in my body is intelligent and knows how to heal itself. My body is always working toward perfect health. I now release any and all impediments to my perfect healing. I learn about nutrition and feed my body only wholesome food. I watch my thinking and think only healthy thoughts. I love my body. I send love to each organ, bone, muscle, and part of my body. I flood the cells of my body with love. I am grateful to my body for all the good health I have had in the past. I accept healing and good health here and now.

Chapter Thirteen

HEALTH

As I work in my garden, lovingly enriching the soil, planting, harvesting, and recycling, I truly feel in tune with the seasons, the weather, the soil, the vegetation, and each and every creature that dwells on the earth. I can take a small section of hard, unproductive earth and slowly transform it into rich loam that will support life in many forms.

Just as we cultivate our gardens, so can we cultivate our minds and bodies to produce healthy, enriched living. One of the essentials to good health is learning to provide quality nutrition for our bodies in the food we eat. It seems that as Americans we have drifted away from healthful eating to the convenience of fast foods. We are the most overweight, sick nation in the Western world. We overeat fatty, processed foods that are full of chemicals. We support the food manufacturers at the expense of our own health. We seem to have forgotten that the cells in our bodies are living, and need living food to grow and reproduce. Life has already provided us with everything we need to feed ourselves and to remain healthy. The simpler we eat, the healthier we'll be.

Exercise is another component of maintaining a healthy body. If we don't exercise at all, then our bones weaken; they require exercise to stay strong. And it doesn't matter what kind of exercise we do. We can start with just a walk around the block, and build up our strength from there. We need to make exercise a regular part of our lives to keep our bodies as supple and flexible as our minds.

But the most important thing to remember in our efforts to be good to our body is to remember to love it. In order to heal ourselves, it is essential to remove the negative beliefs that contribute to an unhealthy physical condition. We need to look into our own eyes in the mirror and tell ourselves how wonderful we are. We need to give ourselves positive messages every time we see our reflection. We don't have to wait until we become thin or build our muscles or lower our cholesterol or reduce our fat ratio. We need to love ourselves right now and listen with love to the needs of our bodies. We deserve to feel wonderful all of the time!

The following letters relate to the topic of health:

Dear Louise,

I am a 52-year-old woman who was diagnosed with fibromyalgia two years ago. My symptoms are all-over muscle pain and chronic fatigue. I am dealing with this condition from a physical, nutritional, emotional, and spiritual point of view, but I would greatly appreciate any additional help you could give me.

I work as a learning specialist at a community college, and I have a beloved husband, children, and grandchildren. However, my spirit is crying out for expression even though I seem helpless to allow it to. My feet cramp and try to push through my skin like a snake sheds its skin. I feel this is essentially a matter of trust, yet I am afraid to let go. Any advice?

Dear One,

From all the research I have done on fibromyalgia, emotional tension seems to be the main cause. Rigid and stiff thinking contributes to stiffness and knots in the muscles. Tension, fear, and holding on result in the body cramping and gripping. I would strongly suggest you join a yoga class.

These exercises could help greatly in teaching you to relax your muscles and your mind. Free your mind from obligations.

You say your spirit is crying out for expression, but you do not say what you would like this expression to be. Your feet are telling you they want to get out and go. Take off your shoes and dance. Run in the grass or in the sand. Have images of yourself flying in the air, free as a bird. Give yourself permission to be free. Take a month off and go somewhere by yourself. Every time you exhale, you trust that your next breath will be there. Apply that same level of trust to taking your next step in life. The whole world is waiting for you. Affirm: I AM ALIVE AND FREE. I DESERVE TO FLY.

Dear Louise,

I'm a 40-year-old woman who came from a background of an alcoholic mother and a verbally and physically abusive father. I began 'inner work' about two years ago. I have a particular problem that I find embarrassing to reveal, yet I know I must if I am to overcome it.

I'm attractive and intelligent, yet why am I 'hurting' myself? I can't remember when it started, but I pick the skin off my feet and often eat the skin. Sometimes I do it till it bleeds. I also have a scalp problem – no matter how often I wash my hair or what special creams and shampoos I use, the scalp peels, and to be honest, I can't wait till it does so that I can start scratching it and peeling it till it bleeds, too.

I read in one of your books that anything to do with the skin relates to a sense of worthiness. I realize that is an issue judging from the state of my living conditions and finances, since I find some way to sabotage my savings every month. I look forward eagerly to your reply.

Dear One,

As a child they picked unmercifully on you. Now you are carrying on the family tradition by picking on yourself. There is a part of you that still believes the old family message that you're 'not good enough and need to be punished.' We are such obedient little children that we will accept almost any 'family message' no matter how confused/unrealistic/stupid it may be. All right, now you have done your penance; you have assuaged your guilt; it is time for this to be over. I absolve you from any further punishment. The curse has been lifted.

Forget the past. From this moment on, I want you to think *only* about what you *do* want. Think thoughts that bring you joy and make you feel good. Your thinking is creating your future. Make it the best future you can imagine. If you find yourself picking, immediately forgive your parents. Affirm: I FORGIVE YOU BOTH, AND I AM FREE TO LOVE MYSELF! Your whole life will change for the better.

Dear Louise,

I have had a hernia in my left groin. The doctors told me that as long as it did not bother me, it was not serious. However, in recent weeks, it has given me some pain at various times, so I decided to have the hernia fixed. When the time came, I got sick and could not have the surgery.

Since then, the same thing has happened several times. I am ready for the surgery and something comes up that blocks me from having it. I cannot understand this, and I am beginning to wonder why. Is there some reason I am not supposed to do it? The first operation was a great success, and I actually thought I was ready for the second one. Would you give me your opinion on this?

Dear One,

When obstacles occur, it usually means that it is not the right time to do something. There is a reason for the delay. Trust that everything is working out for your highest good. I wonder what kind of mental burdens you are carrying? Hernias often represent stress and old mental burdens. How can you lighten the load for yourself. Who do you need to forgive? These would be good issues to consider before you go in for the next surgery. And in the meantime, send love to your body and especially to your stomach and your groin. In your morning meditation, see healing energy flowing through you. Know that you are a divine expression of Life. A good affirmation for you could be: I DIGEST LIFE WITH JOY AND WITH EASE. ALL IS WELL IN MY WORLD.

Dear Louise,

I'm writing to you because I feel lost. My husband of ten years is an alcoholic, and although he has always stopped drinking in the past, this last time it went on for three months, and I chose to separate from him. I tried to make myself stay and accept it, but I couldn't.

I have been having a lot of pain in my arm, my jaw, and just general body pain. I have started meditating, and sometimes this seems to make it worse! I've been doing affirmations and am having a hard time believing that I deserve good in my life. The pain is getting worse, and I feel helpless at times. The doctor wants to put me on antidepressants, and I'd like to know your opinion of them, as I am thinking about them as a last resort. My joints and tendons seem to be getting tighter and more sore. Please give me some advice. I'm getting exhausted.

Dear One,

Thank God you got out. You are not responsible for your husband's drinking, nor can you fix it. Staying there would only destroy you. Congratulations on taking the first step.

Now, get thee to a gym at once. You are filled with anger and rage, and you need to get it out. Exercise is one of the best ways to heal depression. If you can't get to a gym or to a yoga class, then beat the bed with both fists at least once a day and let your feelings out verbally. You need to scream and beat.

Rather than taking a chemical antidepressant use St. John's Wort. St. John's Wort is a natural herbal antidepressant. It can be found in any health food store and has No side effects. St. John's Wort is an herb that has been around forever and is now becoming popular in this country because it is so good at relieving stress and depression.

Go to a 12-step program; Al-Anon would be good. It is filled with people who have to deal with alcoholics. You need love, and you need support. A good affirmation for you would be: I BLESS MY HUSBAND WITH LOVE AND RELEASE HIM, AND I AM FREE TO CREATE A WONDERFUL NEW LIFE.

Dear Louise,

I am a 52-year-old woman who recently had an experience that has literally shattered me. I fell off of a high curb right onto my elbow. Since I have a bit of osteoporosis, the damage was pretty bad. There were multiple fractures, and I had to undergo surgery – pins and a plate were inserted; shattered bone was removed.

Now I am trying to recover, but I have always had an intense fear of doctors, hospitals, and pain. I have to face all three at this time. I also had to leave my job.

Could you give me any words of wisdom to help me through

this healing period. I believe my recovery is slowed down by
fear of physical pain. I'm afraid to do the physical therapy
because it will hurt.

Dear One,

Fear is one of the most incapacitating emotions that we deal with. I feel that you have been running from fear all of your life. I'm sure that this fear came from an early childhood incident. Now you are terrorizing yourself with your thoughts. This is not an act of self-love.

Rescue Remedy, a Bach Flower Essence, which is available at any health food store, would help you calm your nerves at this time. Affirm: EVERY HAND THAT TOUCHES MY BODY IS A HEALING HAND, AND I AM SAFE. This is an affirmation for you to say almost nonstop. You want to quiet down your thoughts. And, be sure to bless your doctors and therapists with love. Music, imagery, and self-hypnosis are also tools that can help you with your healing process. Imagine a pleasant scene during physical therapy, and focus on all the benefits that you will be receiving. Your mind is powerful. Use it for your own good.

Studies have shown that bone loss can be reversed by using a NATURAL progesterone. I encourage you and all women to become truly informed about your bodies. Too much of our information comes from the pharmaceutical companies, which are trying to promote their products. A book I highly recommend is *Women's Bodies, Women's Wisdom*, by Christiane Northrup, M.D.

Dear Louise,

For almost five years now, I've been plagued by low back
pain, which varies in intensity. At times, it is so severe that it
is almost unbearable, and my torso leans to one side. In your

book Heal Your Body, *you say that this could be caused by 'fear of money' or 'lack of financial support.' By this, do you mean that I could be afraid of money, or fear the lack of it?*

Also, this pain is mostly on my right side, and I tend to get breakouts of cold sores and psoriasis on that side of my body. In 1975, I had the fingers of my right hand amputated as the result of an industrial accident. Could there be some kind of cause for this? A pattern of some kind?

One last question: Do affirmations still work even if the person using them is skeptical about whether they work or not? Does faith play a part in healing?

Dear One,

The best place to resolve patterns that are causing pain is in our relationships with our parents. The right side of the body represents the masculine side, and the left side, the feminine. Seeing that almost all of your problems happen on your right side, I would say that there is some deep anger and unresolved issues with your father. Whenever there is pain involved, especially constant pain, as you have, then we are also dealing with long-standing guilt. Yet I am sure there is nothing for you to feel guilty about.

The trouble with holding on to bitterness and resentment from the past is that it can play havoc with our bodies. I know that forgiveness can be difficult, but it is one of the only ways to free ourselves. I feel that you are sitting in this prison of pain that you have unknowingly created.

We often unwittingly allow our minds to dwell on the pain of the past, which can create an atmosphere of negativity around us. This, in turn, attracts negative experiences. I suggest that you find a therapist or a practitioner to help you release these patterns.

Affirmations have been working for you all your life. Every thought you think and every word you speak is an affirmation and is being responded to by Life. In the past, they were often negative and produced negative results. Now, if you choose, your thoughts and words can be positive and forgiving, and your life will change for the better.

Use this affirmation: I ALLOW THE LOVE FROM MY HEART TO HEAL THE PAST, AND I AM FREE.

Dear Louise,
I'm not sure you can help, but my son, who is 27 years old, just started having seizures. The doctors don't know why it is happening. Is there anything you can recommend? Food? Natural healing methods, books to read, exercises to do, etc.? I love my son dearly.

Dear One,
We are now in the second generation of the Great American Diet: junk foods, processed foods, convenience foods. If you read the labels on most foods in the supermarkets, you will realize what we have been putting into our bodies.

I would get your son to a good nutritionist to work in conjunction with your doctor. I am not saying better nutrition is the only answer, but it does play an important part in how we feel. Go to the library and begin to read all about all the natural methods for healing dis-ease. One wonderful book that gives an overview of the different self-healing methods is *Self-Healing* by Louis Proto. I encourage you to explore other healing modalities. See what you can do on those levels.

Know and affirm: MY SON IS A PERFECT CHILD OF THE UNIVERSE, EXPRESSING HIMSELF PERFECTLY.

Louise L. Hay

Dear Louise,

I suffer from terrible halitosis. It's affecting my life in such a way that you can't imagine, especially in my job, where I deal directly with people.

I have already gone to see a gastroenterologist (who didn't find anything wrong) as well as a head, nose, and throat specialist (who thinks everything is mental). I take vitamins, I don't drink or smoke, and I'm in good health otherwise.

I am thinking of seeing an endocrinologist to determine whether something is wrong with my glands, and I would also like to consult with a dental surgeon about whether it could be the metal in my crowns that is producing this bad breath.

Dear One,

Our breath is our life force. It comes from the center of our being and often represents our innermost thoughts. Consistent bad breath could reflect a core issue of resentment or bitterness. If there is an area of your past that needs forgiving, I suggest you begin working on it. You may not know *how* to forgive, but if you declare that you are willing to, the Universe will find a way.

On the physical level, it is good you are consulting your dentist, for decay can often produce unpleasant breath. Perhaps a visit to a periodontist is in order; you might have pyorrhea. Sometimes the teeth and gums need deep scaling to remove offensive breath. Since nutrition plays a larger part in the area of health than most people realize, I also suggest you see a good nutritionist. Too much red meat, sugar, and soft drinks all contribute to gum disease. You may even be allergic to something in your diet.

This could be a good affirmation for you: I RECOGNIZE THE SWEETNESS AT THE CENTER OF MY BEING, AND I EXPRESS IT AT ALL TIMES.

Dear Louise,

Out of the four food groups, I am allergic to two, dairy and fruit, and I don't like meat. I can either eat a whole lot of vegetables or find a way to tame my problem.

I sometimes find myself eating all the things I love, then paying dearly for it. This includes everything from wine and ice cream to cough drops. I'll even use beauty products with a fruit or dairy base. I get extremely high fevers, itch like crazy, and have difficulty breathing. I really overdid it once, and I ended up in the hospital.

I know this must sound like I'm sabotaging myself. And I suppose, at times, I am. I just want to take care of my body the best I can, and if that includes not eating these foods, then so be it. But I will not be satisfied until I have tried everything to end or, at least, control this problem. Any advice you have for me would be greatly appreciated.

Dear One,

First of all, why would you want to eat or use things that are so harmful to your body? To me, your doing that seems very unloving. What happened in the past to make you punish yourself in that way?

If you were born with this allergic reaction, then it is something you have chosen to make peace with in this lifetime. If you weren't born with it, then when did this condition start? What was going on in your life at the time? Is there a situation you must forgive and heal? There is a lesson in this, and you do want to learn it.

For at least a year or two, I suggest you eat only foods that are healing and healthy for you. You can't jump back and forth and continue to feel good. When I had cancer, it seemed as though I had to live on pureed asparagus and sprouts and very little else for months. Yet, I did it, and it was one of the things that contributed to my healing.

I would also recommend that you call 714–523–0800 to see

147

if there is a Nambudripad's Allergy Elimination Techniques (NAET) practitioner in your area. Thousands of patients who could not find relief elsewhere have been successfully treated for both food and environmental allergies by NAET.

Let's make peace with your current situation. You always need to be at peace where you are before you can learn your lesson and move to the next level. A good affirmation for you is: I ENJOY THE FOODS THAT ARE BEST FOR ME, AND THE ANSWERS I NEED COME TO ME WHEN I AM AT PEACE.

Dear Louise,

For most of my life, I was very healthy physically. Then, three years ago (at the age of 43), I became ill and had two operations. During recovery, I discovered your writings and started to do a lot of reading, which I found inspiring. However, the problem is that since those operations, I seem to have developed one health problem after another. There are so many things I want to do in life (artwork, volunteering, spiritual growth), but when I get ill, I do nothing but get depressed. I am no longer living my life, but merely coping with it.

There is a part of me that is convinced that these constant bouts of illness (related to the digestive and reproductive systems) are messages to myself, things that I have caused. The problem is that when I feel ill, I seem incapable of following the spiritual insights I've read about. Surely, if I've brought sickness on myself, I should be able to bring on healing, too, right? But part of me is afraid that if I do things such as affirmations, meditation, etc., and they don't work, I'll be worse than I was before. I'm at a miserable standstill. Can you offer any insights that might help me jump-start my life again.

Dear One,

Affirmations, meditation, and so on can only improve the quality of your life. Please don't add guilt to your burden of illness. The message that I am hearing is: 'I don't deserve to get well.' What parent would you be pleasing/loving by being ill? Did one of your parents get sick around the age of 43 and stay sick? Is this the only way that you can get rest or get out of doing something? These are important questions to ask, for it may be a family pattern.

On the other hand, on a physical level, 43 is about the age that the body fed on junk food or even the standard American diet of processed foods (20 percent sugars and 37 percent fats) is beginning to show the effects of this lack of nutrition. The largest-selling items in supermarkets are sodas, canned soup, processed cheese, and beer. We are the most overweight, sick nation in the Western world. The cells in our bodies are living and, as such, need living foods to grow and reproduce.

We are what we think and what we eat. We need to pay more attention to what we put into our bodies. My philosophy on food is if it grows, eat it; if it doesn't grow, don't eat it. Fruits, vegetables, nuts, and grains grow. Processed foods cannot sustain life no matter how inviting the package. Do visit a good nutritionist, and you may be surprised by the positive results that you can get by changing your diet. Affirm: I AM OPEN AND RECEPTIVE TO THE NEXT STEP ON MY HEALING PATHWAY.

Affirmations for Good Health

I love my body.

My body loves to be healthy.

My blood has life and vitality.

Every cell of my body is loved.

I deserve good health.

I know how to take care of myself.

I am healthier now than I have ever been.

I listen with love to my body's messages.

My health is radiant, vibrant, and dynamic.

I am grateful for my perfect health.

I embrace my inner child with love. I take care of my inner child. It is the child who is frightened. It is the child who is hurting. It is the child who does not know what to do. I will be there for my child. I embrace it and love it and do what I can to take care of its needs. I make sure to let my inner child know that no matter what happens, I will always be there for it. I will never turn away or run away. I will always love this child.

Chapter Fourteen

INNER CHILD

I t doesn't matter how old you are, there is a little child within who needs love and acceptance. If you're a woman, no matter how self-reliant you are, you have a little girl who's very tender and needs help. If you're a man, no matter how macho you are, you still have a little boy inside who craves warmth and affection.

As children, when something went wrong, we tended to believe that there was something wrong with us. Children develop the idea that if they could only do it right, then parents and caregivers would love them, and they wouldn't beat them or punish them. In time the child believes, *There is something wrong with me. I'm not good enough.* As we grow older, we carry these false beliefs with us. We learn to reject ourselves.

There is a parent inside each of us, as well as a child. And most of the time, the parent scolds the child – almost non-stop! If we listen to our inner dialogue, we can hear the scolding. We can hear the parent tell the child what it is doing wrong or how it is not good enough. We need to allow our parent to become more nurturing to our child.

I have found that working with the inner child is most valuable in helping to heal the hurts of the past. At this point in our lives – right now – we need to begin to make ourselves whole and accept every part of who we are. We need to communicate with our inner child and let it know that we accept the part that did all the stupid things, the part that was funny-looking, the part that was scared, the part that was very foolish and silly – every single part of ourselves.

Love is the greatest healing power I know. Love can heal even the deepest and most painful memories because love brings the light of understanding to the dark corners of our mind. No matter how painful our early childhood was, loving our inner child now will help us to heal it. In the privacy of our own minds we can make new choices and think new thoughts. Thoughts of forgiveness and love for our inner child will open pathways, and the Universe will support us in our efforts.

The following letters relate to the topic of our inner child:

Dear Louise,

The manifestation of my problem is being overweight. I know I created it to cope with a rough childhood, but my life is marvelous now. I'm at the end of second-year Science of Mind classes and have learned that I create my life. Why can't I let go of this old way of coping?

Dear One,

I am so glad that you have made some wonderful, positive changes in your life since you came into Science of Mind. Studying and practicing Science of Mind is one of the best and quickest ways to change your life for the better.

However, what you call a 'rough childhood' must have left some deep scars or negative patterns within you. These must be looked at, forgiven, and released. I still hear a note of you scolding yourself for not being good enough. Your problem has always been fear and feeling wrong.

Begin to affirm to yourself: IT IS NOW SAFE FOR ME TO FORGIVE ALL OF MY CHILDHOOD TRAUMAS. I AM FREE OF THE PAST. IT IS NOW SAFE FOR ME TO LOVE MYSELF TOTALLY IN THE NOW.

Keep studying. Keep growing in understanding. Your life will continue to improve. I know you can do it.

Dear Louise,

I was raised by parents who had very little love for themselves or others. They rarely praised me or validated my self-worth. Instead, they continually criticized and berated me, no matter how hard I tried to win their approval. Also, they frequently fought violently with each other, and sometimes my father physically abused my mother, my sisters, and me.

As an adult, I have forgiven my parents for my poor upbringing, but I find it difficult to rid myself of many of the messages they taught me as a child.

Louise, how can I erase negative messages of the past? I need to learn to love myself and to realize my self-worth, but I feel locked in the shame and guilt and fear I was raised with.

Dear One,

So many wonderful workshops are available to you. There are 12-step programs of every sort. Many are listed in the front of your phone book under Community Services. By reaching out and taking advantage of the help they offer, you can place yourself in a healing environment that may be very helpful. You can also go within and silently ask the Universe to bring you to the appropriate next step in your healing process. Be sincere in really desiring to move into greater understanding.

Also, remind yourself every day that guilt is merely the feeling associated with a thought that you did something wrong. Shame is only a feeling associated with a thought that something was wrong with you. Use the affirmation: I AM PERFECT, WHOLE, AND COMPLETE JUST AS I AM.

The more you repeat this statement of truth about yourself, the quicker you will release the past.

Dear Louise,
I want to know if you can give me a helpful affirmation. I suffer from low self-esteem, and I am in therapy. I am concerned about excessive perspiration. I know my problem is deeper than just having healthy sweat glands. I have a lot of problems, but I'm willing to do the work if you will give me guidance. Thank you, Louise, for your books and for being a part of my life.

Dear One,
It sounds as if your body is in a constant state of alarm. When fear becomes chronic and the body is always functioning in a 'fight-or-flight' state, the body produces a constant flood of adrenaline, causing heavy perspiration.

Take the time throughout the day to pause and reassure yourself that you are safe. Fear is often created by a belief from childhood that one is separate and alone in the world. Take time to remind your inner child that you are one with all of life. A wonderful affirmation for you is: I AM SAFE IN THE UNIVERSE, AND ALL LIFE LOVES AND SUPPORTS ME.

Dear Louise,
I am a recent widow trying to understand what it feels like to be a child of God. I can't relate to God's love for his children because I had no father/daughter relationship. My dad was rarely home, and when he was, he never spoke to me, hugged me, or even acknowledged that I was there.

With prayers and meditation, I have been given joys beyond anything I could ever hope for, yet at this time, I feel there is a lost part of myself that deals with this unknown fatherly love. I have even experimented with returning to the child within me, but there is practically no inner dialogue because I do not know how a daughter and father would respond to each other. It is a frustrating situation. Could you please give me some insight or perhaps advise me on how I might tap into knowing the beauty of God's fatherly love?

Dear One,

Although our patriarchal society has always tried to make us think of God as an old man sitting on a cloud taking note of our sins – that is, a father figure relating to his children – this is not true. God is far more than a human figure. I believe 'God' is this incredible intelligence that created all the universes and that also beats your heart and breathes your body each moment. You can love God without making God a human person.

Yes, we are all children of this power that created us, but we do not have to have a physical relationship with our own father to feel this connectedness. Yet, I understand you are feeling the great loss of your husband and also your father.

It is sad that your father's upbringing restricted his ability to demonstrate love. I would imagine his father never spoke to him, and he probably believed that was how parents were supposed to behave. Forgive your father. Have daily conversations with him, and ask him to help you with your understanding of fatherly love. Also know that when it is your time to leave the planet, your father will be waiting for you with love.

A good affirmation for you is: I GIVE MY INNER CHILD ALL THE LOVE IT HAS EVER WANTED AND MORE. MY CHILD IS SAFE AND LOVED. I also highly recommend the book *Self-Parenting*, by John Pollard III.

Louise L. Hay

Dear Louise,

  How do you build self-confidence? How do you trust yourself?

  I was a victim of child abuse and may have also been sexually abused. I attempted suicide at 15 and have been through three marriages. I've done a lot of forgiveness work and no longer blame my parents.

  Since I was a child, I've wanted to become a nurse. I entered a ten-month practical nursing program and was told by my instructor that I tend to hesitate or hold back, but if I could learn to trust myself and take initiative, I would do just fine. She said that I have one of the highest averages in our class, so the theory and knowledge are in my head, I just have trouble applying it.

  I have just finished three weeks on the surgical floor with another instructor. She told me that no one will hire me because I am too slow. Right now, I am on spring break, and there's a part of me that doesn't want to go back to school. I feel hopeless and helpless.

Dear One,

  Being a nurse means taking care of someone. Please remember that you are someone and that you need to begin to take care of yourself first. Nurse yourself in ways that support you. Act as though you are your own patient. Ask yourself: 'What do I want to do for myself?' This will be very healing for you, and as you heal yourself, you will find it easier and easier to give in the ways you want to give.

  When feelings of hopelessness and helplessness come up, realize that you are only dealing with fear. You are not hesitant or slow or holding back. You are just frightened. These old feelings are just the little girl within you coming to the surface. She needs to be comforted and reassured often. Take her by the hand and tell her that you are here for her now and will never allow her to be abused again.

Look in the mirror every morning and evening and affirm: I NOW NURSE MY INNER CHILD WITH ALL THE LOVE I HAVE IN MY HEART, AND SHE IS HEALED.

Inner child work is an ongoing process. Your inner child is always there and is always looking for comfort. It took a little time, but I have healed my wounded inner child, and I know that you can, too.

Affirmations for
Nurturing the Inner Child

I love myself totally in the now.

I embrace my inner child with love.

I am willing to go beyond my own limitations.

I take responsibility for my own life. I am free.

I am grown up now, and
I take loving care of my inner child.

I now go beyond my old fears and limitations.

I am at peace with myself and my life.

I am safe to express my feelings.

I love and approve of myself.

I create my future now.

Children are not the parents' possessions; they are blessings from the Universe. They are individual bright spirits, old spiritual souls coming to have another human experience. They have chosen their parents for the lessons and challenges they will be given. They are here to teach us many things if we are open to learning from them. Children are challenging for they often have different ways of looking at Life. Parents frequently insist on teaching them old, outdated ideas that the children instinctively know are not right for them.

It is the parents' duty to provide a safe, nurturing space for this soul to develop its current personality to the fullest. If we could but realize that each child who comes to this planet is a healer and could do wondrous things to advance humanity if it is but encouraged. When we try to force a child into a mold that was passed down from our grandparents, then we do the child a disservice, and we do society a disservice.

Chapter Fifteen

PARENTING/CHILDREN

I t is vitally important to keep the lines of communication open with children. Often what happens when children start to talk about their likes and dislikes is that they are told over and over again, 'Don't say that. Don't do that. Don't feel that. Don't, don't, don't.' Eventually, children stop communicating and sometimes leave home. If you want to have your children around as you grow older, keep the lines of communication open when they are younger.

Applaud your children's uniqueness. Allow them to express themselves in their own style, even if you think it's just a fad. Don't make them wrong or tear them down. Goodness knows, I have gone through many, many fads in my lifetime, and so will you and your children.

Children never do what we tell them to do; they do *what* we do. We can't say, 'Don't smoke' or 'Don't drink' or 'Don't do drugs' if *we* do them. We have to serve as examples and live the sort of life we want our children to express. When parents are willing to work on loving themselves, it's amazing to see the harmony that is achieved within the family. Children respond with a new sense of self-esteem and start to value and respect who they are. If we can show our children that they are not victims and that it is possible for them to change their experiences by taking responsibility for their own lives, we will begin to see major breakthroughs.

We don't have to be 'perfect parents.' If we are loving parents, our children will have an excellent chance of growing up to be the kind of people we would like to have as friends. They will be individuals who are self-fulfilled and successful. Self-fulfillment brings inner peace. I think the best thing we can do for our children is to learn to love ourselves, for children always learn by example. We will have a better life, and they will have a better life.

The following letters relate to the topic of parenting:

Dear Louise,

My husband and I have very different ideas on how to raise children. We both come from a traditional Christian upbringing, and I realize that my husband has the final say on such matters, but I worry that he is too harsh with our son. We have three children, a boy and two girls. My husband is very loving with the two girls (who are eight and nine), but he is very rough with our son. He is already teaching him how to fight (he's only six years old), and telling him that it is wrong to cry.

I don't like the idea of showing such a difference in how we treat the children. I try to be loving with all three of them. I've read your book You Can Heal Your Life, *and I found it very inspirational. But I don't know how I can use your ideas in this situation. Can you offer any suggestions?*

Dear One,

Why does your husband have the final say on how to raise the children? They have come from your body, and you need to have an equal say. It is time that traditional Christian religions realize that women are equal beings.

I would imagine that your husband is treating your son as he was treated as a child and was raised to believe that this is how to treat boys. In my opinion, this is a form of child abuse and torture. Your boy will either grow up to treat his own children in this way, or he will spend much of his life in

164

therapy. He is also learning to hate women because his sisters are treated well while he is abused.

Fists always equal fear. When children are taught self-esteem, they never have to fight. Now, the best work you can do is in the privacy of your own mind. Let's have your affirmation be: ALL MY CHILDREN ARE TREATED FAIRLY AND LOVINGLY. Then keep seeing your husband as a loving father to all his children, including your son.

Dear Louise,

My 12-year-old son is intelligent, supersensitive, and very low on self-esteem. He's had therapy for eye and coordination problems, but the therapy only seemed to reinforce his view that 'There's something wrong with me.' His typical statements are, 'I'm a nerd,' 'Nobody, likes me,' 'I'm stupid,' and 'I don't do anything right.' He also worries about everything.

I am at a loss as to how to help him, and I am concerned about what this attitude could lead to. I don't seem to get through to him that he is special and not a failure just because he doesn't meet somebody else's expectations.

Dear One,

I believe that each of us selects a particular lesson to learn while we're here on this planet. A baby born with a particular dis-ease or condition has the opportunity to learn to love the self unconditionally.

It sounds like your son may be withdrawn and a loner. What does he believe he's gaining by not participating in the world around him?

You may also want to notice what your son is eating. Nutrition plays a very important part in how we feel. Check with his doctor and teacher for their thoughts as

165

well. Remember, God works through the medical profession, too.

The best and quickest way to get our children to change is to change ourselves. If you want your son to have self-worth and self-love, then you must develop it yourself. Ease up on your son. Learn to love yourself as much as you can, and you will notice positive changes in him. Affirm: THE MORE I LOVE MYSELF, THE MORE MY SON LOVES HIMSELF. WE BOTH BENEFIT.

Continue giving him all the wonderful, unconditional love described in your letter. As much as parents would like, we cannot learn the lessons for our children. All we can do is provide them with the tools.

Dear Louise,

I hope you can help us. My husband is a recovering alcoholic, and I am an adult child of an alcoholic and a recovering alcoholic. Our concern right now is our children. Both suffer from attention-deficit disorder. Our 13-year-old girl is quiet and withdrawn, and she can't function in school. In third grade, she was classified as borderline dyslexic and was put in special classes, but she refused help and became more withdrawn and angry. When she went into the sixth grade, I tried to get her into counseling, but she and my husband fought me. Finally, I washed my hands of her. She was Daddy's girl, and I was tired of being the bad guy. In the eighth grade, she overdosed on drugs the first time she tried them. She's now under a psychiatrist's care.

Our 6-year-old boy started having trouble in preschool. He was hyper and disrespectful. We talked to him and gave him 'time-outs' and spankings, but he's a vengeful child – if one person hurts his feelings, he becomes disruptive and aggressive and claims we don't love him. Now, he's uncontrollable and is on medication at night because he has fits of anger.

*We try to remain positive. Through all this, my husband
and I have gotten closer to each other and God. I try
affirmations every day and affirm that my children are
divinely guided, but at times our faith and strength fail. It
seems too much. What is the belief system causing this
behavior? What can I do to help these kids and to help my
husband and I keep our sanity?*

Dear One,

Open, honest communication seems to be missing in this
family. Are you and your husband both in 12-step programs? Are you in counseling? It seems as though your kids
are now acting out the behaviors you and your husband
used to go through. You ALL need to go to a good marriage
and family counselor. You need help on an ongoing basis for
a while. If the family won't go, it is essential that you go. A
good affirmation for you is: THE HELP I NEED IS ALWAYS
AT HAND, AND WE ARE AT PEACE.

I would also suggest that you go to see a good nutritionist.
Read books, investigate nutrition and the effects that foods
have on the body. I am not saying that it's the only answer,
but I have seen astounding results by applying good nutrition. Your children may have strong allergies to certain
foods or to processed, denatured foods.

Dear Louise,

In your book You Can Heal Your Life, *you write that we
choose our parents. My question is: How does 'choosing our
parents' relate to the action of adoption? In our case, the
reason we adopted is because I am sterile. Did I break 'God's
will,' or was this just an obstacle for me to handle?*

167

Louise L. Hay

Dear One,

I believe that when a child cannot get to a specific parent through birth because of sterility or whatever, he or she will find the channel of adoption. The child you have has chosen you for a parent and was able to find a way to get to you. Be grateful for this wonderful opportunity.

Regarding your sterility, God gave you a beautiful baby. Why do you choose to feel guilty? Don't question it and make a negative out of this experience. By loving yourself and accepting your situation, you will have a happy child and a happy marriage. God's will is for you to be happy and fulfilled. Affirm: I AM A LOVING MOTHER, AND I AM DEEPLY GRATEFUL FOR MY BEAUTIFUL BABY.

Dear Louise,

We recently read your book Heal Your Body *and found your mental patterns for dis-ease to be enlightening. But how do we apply it to children? We both have children with major problems – one with the eyes and the other with the heart. Aren't they too young to be suffering from these sorts of maladies?*

Dear One,

When children have illnesses such as you describe, they are frightened and feel very insecure. Remember, children are much more sensitive to the situations around them than grownups are. As adults, we sometimes forget or do not understand how sensitive some children are and what feelings they are holding within them.

Any problems with the eyes represent a mental pattern of not liking what they see, and the heart represents a great insecurity, such as, 'How will I get my needs met?' Take the time to see the world around your children through their eyes. Are there sensitive situations to which you've become desensitized?

As parents, we can most help our children by learning to love and accept ourselves at a deeper level and to create a lifestyle that brings love, peace, joy, and harmony for us all. As you demonstrate a better life for yourselves, the children will pattern after you. Affirm: AS I FORGIVE THE PAST AND HEAL MYSELF, MY CHILDREN ARE ALSO HEALED.

Dear Louise,

I was born with a common, easily corrected birth defect that wasn't discovered until I was almost two years old. After spending my childhood in hospitals, a body cast, and braces, I find that as an adult with children of my own, I am very bitter and full of anger about it. I don't know why I chose to have that experience, but I do know I want to release this rage and bitterness.

Dear One,

Thank you for reaching out. Your willingness to release the pain of the past has already put you on your healing pathway. Whenever a thought of the past moves through your mind, say to yourself, out loud if you can: I AM WILLING TO FORGIVE. I AM NOW FILLED WITH PEACE AND UNDERSTANDING. I AM HEALED AND WHOLE.

Unfortunately, we are not taught in school how to have relationships or how to be good parents. As parents, we muddle through as best we can, having learned parenthood only from what we saw in our own families. Since children learn by observing their parents, your letting go of bitterness

169

about the past is important; otherwise, you will teach your children to react with bitterness. If you teach them love and forgiveness, they will learn to be loving and forgiving (even of the 'mistakes' they feel you made in raising them).

Affirmations for Parents

I communicate openly with my children.

My children are divinely protected.

I have a loving, harmonious, joyous, healthy family.

My children are safe and secure wherever they go.

I have a loving, peaceful relationship with my children.

My children grow strong and love themselves.

I accept and cherish my children's uniqueness.

I allow my children to express themselves freely.

I love my children, and they love me.

We are all a part of the family of love.

I allow my income to constantly expand, no matter what the newspapers and economists say. I move beyond my present income, and I go beyond the economic forecasts. I avoid listening to people out there telling me how far I can go or what I can do. I easily go beyond my parents' income level. My consciousness of finances is constantly expanding and taking in new ideas — new ways to live deeply, richly, comfortably, and beautifully. My talents and abilities are more than good enough, and it is deeply pleasurable for me to share them with the world. I go beyond any feelings that I do not deserve, and I move into acceptance of a whole new level of financial security.

Chapter Sixteen

PROSPERITY

W hen we use the word *prosperity*, a lot of people immediately think of money. However, there are many other concepts that come under the auspices of prosperity, such as time, love, success, comfort, beauty, knowledge, relationships, and health.

If you are always feeling rushed because there isn't enough time to do everything you want, then you have a lack of time. If you feel that success is beyond your reach, then you are not going to get it. If you feel that life is burdensome and strenuous, then you will always feel uncomfortable. If you think you don't know very much and you're too dumb to figure things out, you will never feel connected to the wisdom of the Universe. If you feel a lack of love and have poor relationships, then it will be difficult for you to attract love into your life. People always think, *Oh, I want to get this and that and whatever*. However, abundance and prosperity is about allowing yourself to accept. When you're not getting what you want, on some level you are not allowing yourself to accept.

Having fear about the issue of money comes from our early childhood programming. A woman at one of my workshops said that her wealthy father had always had a fear of going broke, and he passed on the fear that his money would be taken away. She grew up being afraid that she wouldn't be taken care of. Her lack of freedom with money was tied to the fact that her father manipulated his family through guilt. She had plenty of money all her life, and her lesson was to let go of the fear that she couldn't take care of

herself. Even without all the money, she could still take care
of herself.

Many of us have inherited the beliefs we had when we
were young, but we need to go beyond our parents' limitations and fears. We need to stop repeating their beliefs to
ourselves and begin to affirm that it's okay to have money
and riches. If we can trust the Power within to always take
care of us no matter what, we can easily flow through the
lean times, knowing that we will have more in the future.

The following letters relate to the topic of prosperity:

Dear Louise,

*I am a married man in my early 40s, and I have a beautiful
wife, a baby, a nice home, and a fairly good job. Unfortunately, I never feel satisfied with my finances. I seem to wrap
all of my feelings of self-esteem and contentment around how
much money I make and how big my house is or how expensive
my car or other material belongings are compared with those
of wealthier individuals. Why can't I just appreciate what I
have without always wanting more?*

Dear One,

You are not alone. Many men are raised to believe that
their self-worth is wrapped up in external possessions. Your
father probably felt the same way. Part of your spiritual
growth will be to stop keeping 'score' and find new meaning
in loving yourself and life. I would suggest that you take
three days and go on a camping trip in the woods by
yourself. Connect with trees, vegetation, animals, and the
elements. Ask yourself questions such as: 'How can I go
from competing with others to connecting with life?' 'If I had
no house and no income, how would I find meaning in life?'

'What is *really* important to me?' 'What have I come to teach in this life, and what have I come to learn?'

According to Gail Sheehy in her book *New Passages*, unless you begin to find meaning in your life now, you will enter what could be your Flaming Fifties in discontent. What we call Male Menopause is often a depressed state of mind. Do read her book. It is brilliant. It gives us a blueprint for how we can enter and live our Second Adulthood with passion and power. I firmly believe that we do not have to age the way our parents did. We are pioneers in setting new patterns of living long and glorious lives.

Affirm: I AM DEEPLY GRATEFUL FOR EVERYTHING IN MY LIFE. Say this often, and begin to notice all the little things in the life that we so often take for granted.

Dear Louise,

I am having a terrible time establishing a consistent flow of financial prosperity into my life. I was released from a well-paying job several years ago with a very good severance package. I then decided to make a career change, so I became a commissioned salesperson. After three years of living on almost half of my previous income, I am tired of not having enough. I do not want to live in lack anymore.

I am angry at myself for letting my situation get into this shape. Could you share some ideas with me as to where I can go from here? I'm wondering if I have guilt associated with the money I received as a severance package.

Dear One,

When there is a lack of prosperity in one's life, guilt and a feeling of not deserving always play a big role. Any guilt you feel from receiving your severance package is only guilt from the beliefs you accepted as a child about deserving.

You may want to re-evaluate your parents' ideas about finances and forgive them if they were too limited.

Come back to your own center. You are too scattered in your thinking, dwelling too much on a seeming lack of outer security. Deep at the center of your being is everything you will ever need.

Your goal is to love yourself, not to be angry at yourself. Anger is what I call 'poverty thinking,' because it is wasted energy. Anger at yourself pushes away the prosperity you say you want.

Can you love yourself even though you are making less money than before? Are the outer forms of security so important to your personality? Why? Your soul loves you deeply no matter what your income.

If you can temporarily increase your income, you can also do it consistently. I suggest that you take any one exercise from the prosperity books you have read and do it consistently for six months.

Affirm for yourself: I AM CONSISTENT IN MY LOVE FOR MYSELF, AND LIFE CONSISTENTLY SUPPLIES ALL MY NEEDS IN GREAT ABUNDANCE.

Dear Louise,

Why do so many people connected with metaphysics, such as psychics and healers, charge fees, often large ones? I feel their gifts are intended to be shared to increase the consciousness of anyone who wants them, not just those who can afford them.

Dear One,

People may charge what they feel their services are worth. Just because you see their work as 'metaphysical' doesn't mean they must give up their self-worth. Customers or clients decide whether they wish to pay that amount. It is certainly none of my business what others' fees are.

I do not know what kind of work you do; however, I am sure you would not like to work for nothing. How would you pay your bills? What I hear you saying is that you cannot afford to pay for certain services; therefore, you want them free. But services given free are seldom valued by the recipients. Also, you cannot prosper if you deny others the right to do the same. I rejoice when others prosper, for I know it opens the door for me to do the same.

Let's affirm together: I AM PART OF THE EVER-FLOW-ING ABUNDANCE OF THE UNIVERSE. I JOYFULLY PAY, AND I JOYFULLY RECEIVE.

Dear Louise,

I am a 48-year-old man who has experienced losing things of value all my life, such as property, friendships, and accomplishments. I've been cheated out of payment for work, used by friends, and on and on.

My present home was burglarized twice last year. After the first burglary, I called a very close friend who is a minister and described to him what had happened. I asked how I could unravel the psychological pattern that attracts these happenings into my life. He told me to earnestly ask in prayer for answers, and they would come. Consequently, within three days, Spirit revealed to me that I had a lifelong belief in loss, and that each time a loss occurred, it reinforced that belief.

I immediately began the necessary mental work of spiritual mind treatments and affirmations, and I thought I had conquered this pattern. Why, then, did the second burglary occur? What am I missing? What more can I do to be healed?

Louise L. Hay

Dear One,

How very insightful of you to recognize that you have a lifelong belief in loss. This probably came from experiences in your childhood. The mental work you have done since this insight is good, and you have no doubt cleared much of this pattern; however, lifelong beliefs do not go away overnight. This new burglary shows that there is still work to be done.

Remember: That which belongs to you by right of consciousness cannot be taken from you. What we give out always comes back to us.

Is it possible that you unknowingly steal from people? Perhaps you do not actually steal things (not even paper clips from the office), but you might steal time or respect from people, or even steal from a relationship.

Could you possibly believe that you do not deserve good in life? Perhaps you need to do forgiveness work for the people who taught you to believe in loss.

Go within once again and ask to be shown the answer. Also, forgive the people who took from you. A good affirmation could be: I AM HONEST AND DESERVING, AND MY BELONGINGS AND I ARE SAFE.

Dear Louise,

I have a creative job but can't seem to prosper. I come from a childhood of extreme poverty. I realize now that in order to prosper, I need to change my programmed beliefs. Here are the things I heard all the time as a child: No one from around here ever amounted to much. There is not enough money for anyone. There is no work. Everyone here is very poor. Poverty is spiritually enriching. You will starve to death. You don't matter and no one likes you. Everyone suffers. You can't be any better, have any more, or accomplish anything lasting because you came from here. The ones who've left all got sick and died or have been

178

killed. Everyone always comes home because it's horrible out there. What you want does not matter. We have never had much and never will. Those people out there all want to hurt you. People with money are snobs. You have to stay within your social level.

Some advice on turning these patterns around would be joyfully accepted.

Dear One,

First, it would help if you would do some forgiveness work. Let's affirm together: 'I now forgive all those in my childhood who, in their ignorance, taught me negative and incorrect things about myself. I love my parents, and I now move beyond their old, limiting thoughts. I now declare that these affirmations are my new and true beliefs about myself and about life. I accept them as truth and know I deserve all good in this world.'

Now, let's turn each of your childhood beliefs into a positive affirmation:

- I BREAK PRECEDENT IN MY NEIGHBORHOOD.
- I ALLOW MYSELF TO SUCCEED.
- THERE IS MORE MONEY IN THIS WORLD THAN THERE ARE GRAINS OF SAND.
- I CREATE MORE WORK FOR MYSELF THAN I CAN HANDLE, AND IT IS VERY PROFITABLE.
- GOD LOVES THOSE WHO USE THEIR TALENTS AND ABILITIES TO BECOME RICH IN LOVING WAYS.
- I NOW STARVE ALL MY OLD NEGATIVE BELIEFS. THEY ARE OF NO USE TO ME ANYMORE.
- I DO MATTER – TO MYSELF AND TO LIFE. I AM DEEPLY LOVED AND CHERISHED BY THE UNIVERSE.

- CREATIVE INNER WORK IS AS HONEST AS HARD OUTER LABOR, AND IT OFTEN EARNS MUCH MORE MONEY.
- EVERYONE WHO BELIEVES IN SUFFERING, SUFFERS. I NO LONGER CHOOSE TO BELIEVE IN PAIN.
- I NOW DO EVERYTHING WITH EASE.
- I ALREADY HAVE MORE THAN I HAD BEFORE.
- EVERY DAY, IN EVERY WAY, I AM GETTING BETTER AND BETTER.
- I CAN SHOW OTHERS HOW TO LIVE GRANDLY AND GRACIOUSLY.
- I AM ABLE TO PROSPER ON MY OWN.
- I AM MYSELF, AND I MAKE MY OWN RULES.
- IF ONE LOOKS FOR HORROR, ONE FINDS HORROR. I FIND ONLY GOOD WHEREVER I GO AND WHEREVER I LOOK.
- I AM AT HOME IN THE UNIVERSE.
- THE UNIVERSE RESPONDS TO WHAT I WANT AS LONG AS I BELIEVE I DESERVE IT.
- MY LIFE DOES HAVE MEANING.
- I DO NOT LOOK TO THE PAST TO TELL ME ABOUT THE FUTURE.
- I NOW DESERVE AND HAVE ALL I DESIRE.
- ALL PEOPLE HAVE ONLY MY BEST INTERESTS AT HEART. I AM SURROUNDED BY LOVE.
- ALL THE PEOPLE I KNOW WHO HAVE MONEY ARE KIND, LOVING, AND DOWN-TO-EARTH.
- AS PART OF MY PROSPERITY GROWTH, I AM FREE TO MOVE FROM ONE SOCIAL LEVEL TO ANOTHER SOCIAL LEVEL WITHOUT GUILT OR FEAR.

Many people have negative beliefs about prosperity and money. These are beliefs they learned as children but now that they're adults, they can change these beliefs to better their lives. I was born into a poor family, but I managed to move past that. Today, I experience prosperity in all areas. Here are more affirmations for you. It would help to write them on a piece of paper and keep them in areas where you will see them often.

- TODAY I AM WEALTHY. IT IS ALL RIGHT IF MY FAMILY AND CHILDHOOD FRIENDS CONTINUE TO BELIEVE IN LIMITING THOUGHTS. THEY DO NOT HAVE TO GROW IN THE SAME WAY I AM GROWING.
- I NOW DO THE WORK I LOVE, AND I AM WELL PAID FOR IT. I KNOW HOW TO KEEP AND SAVE MONEY. I DESERVE TO HAVE MONEY IN THE BANK, AND I ACCUMULATE IT NOW. ALL MY BILLS ARE PAID, AND I HAVE MONEY TO SPARE.
- WHEN I FEEL OVERWHELMED BY CIRCUMSTANCES AROUND ME, I RECOGNIZE THAT THESE ARE ONLY OLD PATTERNS COMING UP. I QUIETLY GO WITHIN AND ASK MYSELF, 'WHAT IS BEST FOR ME?' ALL CONFUSION THEN LEAVES ME, AND I BECOME CLEAR WITH REGARD TO THE STEP I OUGHT TO TAKE.
- THE CHILD IN ME NO LONGER CHOOSES TO BELIEVE THAT SOMEONE WILL INEVITABLY TAKE ADVANTAGE OF ME. AS I RELEASE THIS RIDICULOUS BELIEF, IT DISAPPEARS BACK INTO THE NOTHINGNESS FROM WHENCE IT CAME.

Read these affirmations morning and night for at least a month or two. You can change your world by changing your thoughts. Stick with it, and you will win.

Louise L. Hay

Dear Louise,

I am a 35-year-old woman who has been living the life of a struggling artist for ten years. When I'm drawing and painting, I feel alive, involved with the world, at one with the universe. However, I've only enjoyed modest success in my field. In order to pay the rent and buy groceries, I've had to hold a variety of jobs, including waiting on tables and doing clerical work.

Although I'm quite good at these supplemental jobs, I have found that they take more and more of my energy until I really don't have very much left within myself to devote to my art. I find myself questioning my path. The struggles are getting old, and at times I feel jealous of those who have achieved the degree of success I strive to attain. I sometimes think about giving up art altogether in favor of a more traditional and lucrative job, but I really don't think I could do it and still be myself.

Can you give me some direction?

Dear One,

Jealousy always comes from scarcity. We want to know that there is plenty for everyone, including ourselves. I wonder if you are buying into some childhood message that says: 'Artists always struggle. Art is a foolish way to make a living. You do not deserve to succeed. Only men can succeed in art. Life is difficult, and you have to work hard.'

I think somewhere in you there are old messages that deny you success. Please make a few lists: What I believe about art; what my parents believed about art; what I believe about success, about women, about deserving, about energy, about struggling. Turn every negative statement into a positive affirmation.

Give up the mental struggle inside of you. Begin to allow yourself to totally enjoy your life as it is today. Be grateful and thankful for your creative talents. The universe loves gratitude. Rejoice in the success of others. Make everything you do fun and creative. Love yourself and love your life. You are now moving to the next level. All is well. Affirm: I RADIATE SUCCESS, AND I PROSPER WHEREVER I TURN.

Affirmations for Attaining Prosperity

Prosperity is my Divine Right.

I am constantly increasing my
conscious awareness of abundance,
and this reflects in a constantly increasing income.

My good comes from everywhere and everyone.

I prosper wherever I turn.

I deserve and willingly accept an
abundance of prosperity flowing through my life.

I now establish a new awareness of success.

I know I can be as successful
as I make up my mind to be.

I rejoice in the successes of others,
knowing there is plenty for us all.

All my needs and desires are met before I even ask.

Prosperity of every kind is drawn to me.

Relationships are wonderful, and marriages are wonderful, but they're all temporary because there comes a time when they end. The one person I am with forever is me. My relationship with me is eternal. So I am my own best friend. I spend a little time each day connecting with my heart. I quiet down and feel my own love flowing through my body, dissolving fears and guilt. I literally feel love soaking into every cell in my body. I know that I am always connected to a Universe that loves me and everyone else unconditionally. This unconditionally loving Universe is the Power that created me. As I create a safe place in myself for love, I draw to me loving people and loving experiences. It is time to let go of my stuff about how relationships are supposed to be.

Chapter Seventeen

ROMANTIC RELATIONSHIPS

Being 'needy' is the best way to attract an unsuccessful relationship. If you expect the other person to 'fix' your life or be your 'better half,' you are setting yourself up for failure. You want to really be happy with who you are before you enter a relationship. You want to be happy enough so that you don't even need a relationship to be happy.

Similarly, if you have a relationship with someone who does not love himself or herself, then it is impossible to really please that person. You will never be 'good enough' for someone who is insecure, frustrated, jealous, self-loathing, or resentful. Too often we knock ourselves out trying to be good enough for partners who don't have any idea how to accept our love – because they don't know who they are. Life is a mirror. What we attract always mirrors those qualities we have, or beliefs we have about ourselves and relationships. What others feel about us is their own limited perspective of life. We must learn that Life has always loved us unconditionally.

As you work on resolving the blocks that stand between you and your relationship, practice being your own lover. Treat yourself to romance and love. Demonstrate to yourself how special you are. Pamper yourself. Treat yourself to small acts of kindness and appreciation. Buy yourself flowers; surround yourself with colors, textures, and scents that please you. Life always mirrors back to us the feeling we have inside. As your inner sense of love and romance grows, the right person to share in your increasing sense of intimacy will be attracted to you like a magnet. Most important, you will not have to give up any part of your own self-intimacy to be with that person.

The following letters relate to the topic of romantic relationships:

Dear Louise,

Why don't we have a 'divine model' of the perfect couple? Why didn't God send us a sample? The examples that we have, such as Jesus Christ, Buddha, Mother Teresa, Sai Baba, and so on, were all alone. Yet, they are the ones teaching us about love. Is there anything wrong with romantic love? Is romantic love only an invention of our ego? I need a good affirmation to help me find all the answers.

Dear One,

You will never find 'all the answers,' for Life is far greater than our human minds can comprehend. Stretching to understand more and more of life is a worthy endeavor. You ask a good question; there is much to ponder here. I am sure other readers will have their own answers. Here are some of my thoughts:

Remember that anyone who is a spiritual leader on the level of the people you mention has chosen that path as a full-time job and has very little time left for family living. So far, it would seem that humankind has not chosen to create this model. God has nothing to do with it. If we want this 'divine model,' then it is up to us to create it. Perhaps the next Messiah will be a woman and will choose a man as her partner. (For women who would like to explore a feminine look at religion, I recommend the book *A GOD WHO LOOKS LIKE ME: Discovering a Woman-Affirming Spirituality*, by Patricia Lynn Reilly.)

Romantic love is wonderful. Everyone's life needs to be touched by it. Yet, there is so much more to love than just romance. This unconditional love is the kind of love most of these teachers want the rest of humanity to learn. Each morning I use the affirmation: LET MY UNDERSTANDING DEEPEN TODAY SO THAT I CAN COMPREHEND MORE OF LIFE.

Dear Louise,

I am a 43-year-old woman, and I am still single. I've said affirmations about my wonderful, loving husband manifesting in my life, and I've joined numerous singles groups, etc., but still nothing.

I have decided to remain chaste until I find my perfect mate, but the last four years of my life have been the longest and loneliest of my life. I haven't been held or kissed; however, I'm honoring the sacred nature of my sexuality by staying chaste. I keep wondering if God is hearing my prayers or if I'm going to have to get used to living alone forever. The thought of this possibility brings me to tears, and I can't imagine how I will endure this. Should I stop saying my affirmations for a loving relationship? Do I just give up?

Dear One,

I understand your desire and longing for bringing the perfect mate into your life to share your love with. You are not alone in this. However, at the moment, you do not have someone. And *you* are making yourself miserable. I too would love to have a loving mate in my life, *and* I do not have one. I too have not been kissed in four years, *yet* they have *not* been the loneliest years of my life. I have often been hugged because I hug many, many people. My life is rich and full because I make it that way. I have compassion for

189

you, and I know you do not have to suffer in this way. You are not being punished by God or by Life.

Yes, continue to do affirmations for a loving relationship *and* expand your affirmation to include lots of love in your life. Affirm for joy and happiness. Affirm for fulfillment. Affirm for doing work that helps heal the planet. Do some volunteer work; get out and help others. Expand your life. Give love to others. Be grateful and appreciative for all the good you do have in your life. Have *fun*! Life is here to be enjoyed.

Dear Louise,

I am a man in my 40s who was married for 13 years when I was much younger, and I have now been divorced for 15 years. I am currently involved with a loving, beautiful woman whom I've been seeing for over three years now. Although I love her, whenever she brings up the subject of marriage, I feel enormous resistance – both to the idea of any type of commitment and to the idea of a legal union.

The idea of being financially responsible for someone else 'forever' frightens me. However, it's my feeling that my girlfriend expects an answer to the marriage question in the very near future, and I don't know what to do. I fear that I will either lose her by initiating a breakup that I don't really want (which will hurt her terribly), or that she will eventually lose patience with my indecision. Can you help me deal with my conflicting feelings?

Dear One,

Tell the truth. Explain exactly how you feel and why. Show her your letter if it's hard to bring the subject up. You must be able to communicate if you want to have a good relationship. If you both can't talk about things, then you are in trouble. If you believe you love this lady, then perhaps you will be willing to get some counseling. Have a trained person help you look at all the issues involved. There is much more going on here than you are aware of.

You are doing what so many people do. You are looking at the past to tell you what the future will be like. It sounds like the first marriage was not a good one and you were glad to get out. You are not the same person you were then, and this is not the same situation.

Affirm: I RELEASE THE PAST, AND I LIVE IN THE NOW. Bless that last relationship, and let it go!

Dear Louise,

I have a relationship with a man I am in love with, although I cannot call it a loving relationship. He knows about my feelings for him but claims he is not ready to be with a woman right now because of his 'bad past experiences with women,' as he puts it. Still, when we are alone or with others, he behaves as if we are a couple. He has many great qualities, but he is also quick-tempered and sometimes rough or rude with other people and also with me.

I would really like to find a way to communicate with him, not only because of my feelings for him, but also because I simply enjoy his company. I would like to deal with him in a relaxed, joyous way, but I am in a state of confusion and do not know how I should act.

My relationship is suspended now, which is what I decided to do after his 'rough period.' What should I do to keep this relationship, but put it into better shape than it is now?

Dear One,

The first thing you need to do is read the book *Women Who Love Too Much* by Robin Norwood. It offers a perfect

191

picture of what you are doing. What you are calling 'love' is an addiction to an abusive relationship. You appear to be caught in the old bind of thinking you can change a man if you love him enough. It never works. The next step in this relationship is for him to become physically abusive to you.

You still have much work to do on loving yourself and building your self-esteem. Probably your childhood experiences made you feel you had little self-worth. *I NOW DEVELOP A DEEP FEELING OF SELF-WORTH AND SELF-ESTEEM* would be a good affirmation for you. I know you can be much more than you think.

Dear Louise,

Six weeks ago I told my fiancée that I felt unable to handle all the pain she triggered in me and I wanted to call off our wedding and our relationship. I've been wishy-washy about this relationship from the beginning and just wanted her to release me from the commitment.

However, after six weeks of not seeing her, I've still not been able to go on with my life, and for some unknown reason I want her back — even while feeling she is just not right for me. She has a lot of anger and resentment from her previous marriage, which she has not been able to totally release. She vents it on me at times, and I just can't tolerate her doing that.

Dear One,

The ending of a relationship is difficult for most of us to handle. We often give our power over to the other person, feeling that he or she is the source of the love we feel. Then, if that person leaves, we are devastated. We forget that love lies within us. We have the power to choose our feelings.

Remember, no person, place, or thing has any power over us. Bless her with love and release her.

Some of us are so starved for love that we will endure a poor relationship just to be with someone, anyone. We all need to develop so much self-love that we only attract to ourselves people who are there for our highest good.

We must all refuse to accept abuse of any sort. To accept it only tells the Universe that such is what we believe we deserve, and as a result, we will get more of it. Affirm for yourself: I ONLY ACCEPT KIND AND LOVING PEOPLE IN MY WORLD.

Dear Louise,

There has been a serious debate in recent years about man/woman relationships, and I have pondered this problem myself. Why do some men like women who treat them like dirt? No matter what nice person comes along, these men find some excuse to reject kindness and love. It has been said that mistreated women lack self-esteem, yet men's self-esteem is not as widely addressed as women's. What is your view on this?

Dear One,

If your mother treated you like dirt, then unfortunately you would associate this treatment with love. When you grow up you look for women who will treat you as your mother did. A nice woman would make you feel uncomfortable and even unloved. It is the same with women who were abused by their fathers during childhood. They often unconsciously gravitate toward a man who will continue this abuse.

This is why forgiveness work is so important. It is not to say that what happened in the past was okay, but to free ourselves from being in a prison of resentment and bitterness. I know I had far too many years of living in self-pity and resentment. It wasn't until I could forgive the past that I could begin to create a good life for myself. Resentful, self-pitying thoughts cannot create joy in our lives.

So you see we all have comfort zones in our relationships with others. These comfort zones are formed when we are very young. If our parents treated us with love and respect, then we came to associate this type of treatment with being loved. If, as for many of us, our parents were unable to treat us with love and respect, we learned to be comfortable with this lack. We associate being treated badly with being loved. This becomes the pattern we use unconsciously in all our relationships.

This dysfunctional belief pattern – that being treated badly equals love – is not exclusive to either gender. However, it is more widely recognized in women because, culturally, women are encouraged to express vulnerability and are, as a result, more willing to admit when their lives are not working. This is changing, however, as more and more men become willing to reconnect with their vulnerability. An affirmation for all of us is: I OPEN MY HEART TO LOVE.

Dear Louise,

About a year ago, I found out that my husband had been seeing another woman. She has since moved away, but the whole situation caused me great emotional pain, loss of trust, and lack of confidence in myself. My husband claims now that I am not his 'type' and feels stuck in the relationship. (Our religious beliefs prohibit divorce.) Incidents come up where he clearly shows me that another woman is more appealing to him and that he does not want to be in this relationship. I have been working on myself, but when I am with him, I always feel like I am not good enough and lose any headway that I have made. Should I see a counselor? My husband has rejected any books about marriage or positive thinking and is not interested in counseling.

I am not bad-looking and have many good traits, and I know that other men could appreciate having me as a wife.

Dear One,

With all the challenges you are facing right now, the main issue is still for you to continue working on yourself. You are the only person who needs changing. Build confidence in yourself. Know that you are a perfect being. Don't try to win someone else's love – it doesn't work that way. Stop looking to your husband for approval. Love yourself, and you will attract love in all aspects of yourself.

Once you begin to change, the people around you will see the changes and do the same. Your husband may or may not change as he notices changes in you. That's up to him. This does not make him a 'bad person.' You may simply not be meant for each other at this time.

In regard to being stuck in a no-win situation, when we are children, we have no say in choosing our religious beliefs. However, as adults, if we examine the various religions, we find some that are very supportive of the individual and many that have rigid rules that put limitations on people. If you were to choose a religion today, would you choose one that condemns you to stay with a person who does not want you? Isn't it better to be supported in spirituality in order to become all that you can be?

Of course, see a counselor. He or she will help guide you in your growth process, as well as provide a good ear with which to listen. As you make your inner choices, you will notice people reacting differently to you, including your husband. A good affirmation for you could be: I AM A

Louise L. Hay

BEAUTIFUL, LOVING BEING, AND EVERY DECISION I
MAKE IS FOR MY OWN GOOD.

Dear Louise,
I am a 25-year-old man who is considered handsome by
most people. Yet, every time I approach a woman, she seems
to turn off to me. I am not overbearing – that is, I don't make
overly flirtatious or lewd remarks. I usually say something
like, 'I think you're really beautiful, and I'd like to meet you.'
Isn't this something a woman would want to hear? Why
haven't I been able to connect with anyone? I am an only child
who was raised by my father, and I am wondering if I just
never got used to communicating with women. Any words of
advice?

Dear One,
There is obviously a negative vibration that you give off to
women. I don't think behavior – that is, what you do or say –
has much to do with it. Have you ever done any work on
forgiving your mother for leaving you? What is your father's
attitude toward women? Why did he never remarry? Also,
make a list of all the things that you believe about women.
Take two or three days to do this. Then look at all the
negative beliefs you have about them. You may be surprised
to find some inner beliefs that would deny you a relationship.
I suggest that you join an Al-Anon meeting for a while.
You may learn a lot about yourself. Good affirmations for
you might be: I AM WILLING TO HEAL THE PAST, and
WOMEN LOVE ME.

Affirmations for Creating
Healthy Romantic Relationships

I open my heart to love.

It is safe for me to express love.

I am safe and secure in my love for myself.

I always have the perfect partner in my life.

I am open and receptive to a
wonderful, loving relationship.

Deep at the center of my being,
there is an infinite well of love.

I have come here to learn that there is only love.

I am in a harmonious relationship with life.

I rejoice in the love I have to share.

I am creating lots of room in my life for love.

I grow spiritually when I accept responsibility for my life. This gives me the inner power to make the changes in myself that I need to make. Spiritual growth is not about changing others. Spiritual growth happens to the person who is ready to step out of the victim role into forgiveness and a new life. None of this happens overnight. It is an unfolding process. Loving myself opens the door, and being willing to change really helps.

Chapter Eighteen

SPIRITUAL WELL-BEING

Deep at the center of our being there is an infinite well of love, an infinite well of joy, an infinite well of peace, and an infinite well of wisdom. This is true for each and every one of us. Yet how often do we get in touch with these treasures within us? Do we do it once a day? Once in a while? Or are we totally unaware that we have these infinite treasures?

These treasures are part of our spiritual connection and are vital to our well-being. Body, mind, and spirit – we need to be balanced on all three levels. A healthy body, a happy mind, and a good, strong spiritual connection are all necessary for our overall balance and harmony. One of the major benefits of a strong spiritual connection is that we can live wonderful, creative, fulfilling lives. And we will automatically release so many burdens that most people carry.

We will no longer need to be fearful or carry shame and guilt. As we feel our oneness with all of life, we will drop anger, hatred, prejudice, and the need to be judgmental. As we become one with the healing power of the Universe, we will no longer need illness. And, I believe we will be able to reverse the aging process. Burdens are what age us; they drag down our spirits.

We need to practice getting in touch with our inner treasures on a daily basis. For the truth of our being is that we are filled with unconditional love, and people living the truth can change the world. We are filled with incredible joy. We are filled with serene peace. We are connected to infinite wisdom. What we need to do is to know it and live it. Today we are mentally preparing for tomorrow. The thoughts we think, the words we speak, and the beliefs we accept *do* shape our tomorrows.

Remember, our spiritual connection does not need a middle man such as a church, a guru, or even a religion. We can pray and meditate quite easily by ourselves. Churches and gurus and religions are nice if they are supportive of the individual. Yet, it is important to know that we all have a direct pipeline to the source of all life. When we are consciously connected to this source, our life flows in wondrous ways.

The following letters relate to the topic of spiritual well-being:

Dear Louise,

Could you explain some of your views on karma for me? That is, do you believe that everything that happens to people is caused by something bad that they've done in this life or a past one? Or do you think that 'new karma' can be perpetrated upon someone?

For example, when I hear about a little girl being brutally raped and murdered, I have to wonder how this can be — certainly that little soul hasn't been guilty of anything in this life, could she?

Also, do you think that all souls are redeemed at some point, even someone like Hitler? I'd really be interested in hearing your views on this matter.

Dear One,

First of all, I don't think we ever do anything 'bad.' When you look into the upbringing of some of the most brutal people, including Hitler, you will find a horrendous childhood. This is not to condone that behavior, but to understand that cruelty begets cruelty. Look at the things going on in the Middle East, where children are raised to hate children in other nations. It is no wonder that these nations are constantly at war. Until we learn the lessons of love, we will always be stuck in pain.

I do not know for certain that we carry over karma from lifetime to lifetime. Yet, that is my personal belief. It makes so much sense to me and explains much of the unexplainable, such as child abuse or murders of children. I have often thought that my own childhood abuse could have occurred because I was abusive of children in another lifetime and I needed to know how that felt.

Remember, many questions in Life are beyond our current understanding. That is part of our spiritual learning, to continually expand our understanding of this magnificent experience called Life. No soul has ever been harmed and therefore does not need redemption. It is our personalities that need to be reminded that we are spiritual beings having a human experience, not the other way around.

As we grow spiritually, we see the perfection of all of life. The Universe waits in smiling repose for us to learn that loving unconditionally is the best way to live and will bring us peace, power, and riches beyond our current imagination. Affirm: I DO MY BEST TO HELP CREATE A LOVING, HARMONIOUS WORLD.

Dear Louise,

I have worked in a battered women's shelter for over two years. I have done everything I can not to let this experience affect my spirituality. I've used positive affirmations and have tried to see good or God beyond these experiences. However, every day I get more negative spiritually. I have even turned in my resignation because I just can't go to work anymore.

Louise L. Hay

I need help to stop the downward spiral I am in. I believe that I was spiritually progressing before I took this job, but I can't even seem to get back to my former level. Any insights or tools you could give me would be much appreciated.

Dear One,
How wonderful that you have given your time to help battered women. It is not necessary that you do it forever. Remember, your spirituality has nothing to do with someone else's patterns. You have seen at close hand what lack of self-love and self-esteem can do to a human being.

I have the feeling that you kept trying to 'fix' these women, and therefore you felt like a helpless failure. You can only give love and information. Each person is under the law of their own consciousness, and when they are ready to change and grow, they will.

Be kind to yourself and give yourself a break. Don't use someone else's negativity as an excuse to deny your own spiritual connection to life. Go work where you can find joy. A good affirmation for you could be: I AM A BEAUTIFUL PERSON ENJOYING LIFE. I SURROUND MYSELF WITH OTHER LIKE-MINDED SOULS.

Dear Louise,
Basically, I'm writing because I'm tired of feeling anxious, overly self-critical, and overly concerned with what others think. I am a 28-year-old female who considers herself spiritual — I practice daily affirmations; I don't smoke, drink, or do drugs; and I have strong moral values. However, I feel that I keep getting in the way of my attainment of true inner peace.

Even though I know that I have many things going for me (health, education, supportive parents, etc.), I am somewhat afraid of life, afraid of 'going out there' on my own. I feel that my search for employment has been affected by these feelings, as well as some of my friendships. I have wondered if perhaps the anxiety may be partially due to some physiological cause or nutritional deficit.

I would greatly appreciate any advice you may have, as well as an affirmation that is fitting for my particular situation. Thank you for your help.

Dear One,

You are listening to your ego. Your ego will always try to keep you anxious, fearful, and believing that you are 'not good enough.' The more you criticize yourself, the happier your ego it. Please remember, you are not your body, your emotions, or your problems. You are a spiritual being having a human experience. That which you call 'I' can never be harmed and is eternal.

It is time for you to quiet the negative chatter of your ego. On a daily basis, give yourself time to listen to your own inner wisdom, your Higher Self. No person can be totally in touch with the plethora of knowledge within them without taking time each day to meditate. Sitting in silence is one of the most valuable things we can do.

Continually affirm the truth for yourself: I AM A DI-VINE, MAGNIFICENT EXPRESSION OF LIFE. EVERY-THING I NEED TO KNOW IS REVEALED TO ME. EVERYTHING I NEED COMES TO ME. I AM DIVINELY PROTECTED AND GUIDED EVERY MOMENT. I AM SAFE AND ALL IS WELL IN MY WORLD. I LOVE LIFE AND LIFE LOVES ME. When the negative chatter begins, just say to it: 'Stop!' Then repeat your knowledge of the truth of your being.

Louise L. Hay

Dear Louise,

My daughter and her family live in the San Francisco area, over a fault line. I have often expressed my concern for their welfare, considering the threat of earthquakes and the prophecies concerning that area, and I have encouraged them to relocate.

My daughter's philosophy is that so much negative thought energy focused on possible cataclysms could cause a self-fulfilling prophecy to occur. She feels that if she maintains a positive attitude, she and her family will somehow be protected.

However, my contention is that the forewarnings are already in place and not to act upon them is utter foolishness — God has done His part; she must do hers. If she chooses to remain in a potentially dangerous area, that is her right, but does she have the right to jeopardize the welfare of her young children? I'd appreciate your views on this subject.

Dear One,

I understand your concern for your daughter and her family. And I encourage you to stop wasting your mental energy worrying. There are too many people out there at the moment selling fear and putting negative energy into the atmosphere. Our mind is our most precious tool. What we do with our thoughts can heal or destroy our bodies and our world. Every thought you think is either enhancing or depressing your immune system. You are the one who is in danger. You will make yourself sick if you don't stop this. Also, you don't want to make your daughter dread your phone calls.

Why are you giving so much energy to ancient prophecies? Don't you realize that the whole point of the New Thought wave of consciousness is to defuse those prophecies? Get on the bandwagon of healing ourselves and the planet. You want to use your energy to help heal the planet.

Do daily visualizations of the whole world, including your family, moving into a new dimension of peace and security and plenty for everyone. Meditate on peace, and get a greater understanding of God. God is not a vengeful man. God is a *Universal* Intelligence that goes far beyond the confines of our tiny speck of a planet. You are safe, and so am I.

You need to make peace in your own heart. Begin to trust the Process of Life. Know that the Intelligence of the Universe dwells within your daughter and each member of her family. If it is right for them to move, then this Intelligence will see to it that they do. Know and affirm that ALL OF MY FAMILY IS DIVINELY PROTECTED AT ALL TIMES.

Dear Louise,

I love all animal life and would, in fact, rather spend time with them than with humans. I hold a very negative view of the human race as a whole, and basically feel that most people are selfish, greedy, evil, manipulative, etc.

What troubles me is the question of soul and immortality with respect to animal life. How can it be that humans, with all their faults, weaknesses, and shortcomings, can go to a place called heaven, but animals cannot? Humans are guilty of committing great acts of cruelty against innocent animals. Even though we now have many groups that speak for the welfare of animals, I feel that we have a long way to go.

What I'd like to know is: Where do animals go when they die? Do they have spirits? How do karma and reincarnation figure into this? Since I view animals as the most oppressed life-form on earth, I'd be interested in hearing your views on this matter.

Dear One,

It sounds as if you had a childhood where you were surrounded by selfish, greedy, manipulative people. Where else would you get this outlook on life? We all need to forgive our families for something before we can truly love ourselves. Remember, what we believe about life and what we look for in life, we will always find. Begin each morning by looking for the good within yourself. Find something positive, and then spend the rest of the day seeing that same quality in others. I see my world as populated with loving, giving, supportive people; and also some very unhappy people who create problems for themselves and others out of ignorance. Humanity is awakening as fast as we allow ourselves to find our own pathways.

I, too, love all animals. I have four dogs, two rabbits, and a flock of birds and other wildlife that I feed. Heaven and hell, to me, are not places we 'go' after we die, but places we inhabit here on earth. I believe that animals have a soul or spirit and are also on an evolutionary pathway. Awakened individuals would never harm anyone, including innocent animals. So, let's do our best to come from a loving view of everything and everyone on earth. Also include in your prayers that the awakening of humanity is speeding up. Affirm: I ENVISION A WORLD OF LOVE AND KIND-NESS, AND I DO MY BEST TO CONTRIBUTE TO THIS LOVING WORLD.

Affirmations for Spiritual Well-being

The power that created the world beats my heart.

I have a strong spiritual connection.

Life supports me at every turn.

I feel at one with all of life.

I believe in a loving God.

I trust life to be there for me.

I have a special guardian angel.

I am divinely guided and protected at all times.

I am always progressing on the path of spiritual growth.

I am connected with Divine Wisdom.

I am now willing to see the magnificence of me. I now choose to eliminate from my mind and life every negative, destructive, fearful idea and thought that would keep me from being the magnificent woman that I am meant to be. I now stand up on my own two feet, and support myself and think for myself. I give myself what I need. It is safe for me to grow. The more I fulfill myself, the more people love me. I join the ranks of women healing other women. I am a blessing to the planet. My future is bright and beautiful.

Chapter Nineteen

WOMEN'S ISSUES

W e all need to be very clear that the love in our lives begins with us. So often we look for 'Mr. Right' to solve all our problems, in the form of our fathers, our boyfriends, our husbands. Now it is time to be 'Ms. Right' for ourselves. To do that we need to look honestly at our flaws – not looking at what is wrong with us, but looking for the barriers we have put up that keep us from being all we can be. Many of those barriers are things we learned in childhood, but if we learned them once, we can unlearn them now.

Inner self-esteem and self-worth are the most important things women can possess. And if we do not have these qualities, then we need to develop them. When our self-worth is strong, we will not accept positions of inferiority and abuse. No matter where we came from, no matter how abused we were as children, we can learn to love and cherish ourselves today. As women and mothers, we can teach ourselves to develop a sense of self-worth, and then we will automatically pass this trait on to our children. Our daughters will not allow themselves to be abused, and our sons will have respect for everybody, including all the women in their lives.

Building up women does not mean having to diminish men. Male bashing is as bad as female harassment. We don't want to get into that. Blaming ourselves or men for all the ills in our lives does nothing to heal the situation, and only keeps us powerless. The best thing we can do for the men in our world is to stop being victims and get our own acts together. We want to come from a loving space in our hearts and see everyone on this planet as someone who needs love. When women get it together, we will move mountains, and the world will be a better place in which to live.

The following letters explore women's concerns:

Dear Louise,

I am a 37-year-old woman who has been diagnosed with an irregular heartbeat – that is, there are lapses between the beats that seem like a 'gallop.' The effect is that I feel uncomfortable, especially when winding down in the evening.

After reading your wonderful book You Can Heal Your Life, *I truly believe I can heal this small but irritating ailment, and I suspect that there might be some personal work to be done and lessons to be learned. But after months of work, I find myself stuck.*

The funny thing is, I have never been happier in my personal life. I quit my job of 15 years and am now able to stay home with my three kids. Since you have associated the heart with love and joy, I wonder if too much joy could cause a heart problem. The other side of this change, of course, is that I faced reduced finances and the pressures associated with attempting a new career as a writer. Do you have any suggestions for a way to heal myself?

Dear One,

There is no such thing as too much joy. There may be an old childhood message within you that says, 'You can't have it all,' or 'Don't be too happy,' or 'You are asking for trouble.' Think about the things your parents used to say about happiness, and see if there are some limitations there. Do you really feel you *deserve* to be happy?

As a woman, you need to find your inner center and truly develop your self-esteem and self-worth. When we women learn to love and cherish ourselves, we will be able to move mountains. Remove all pressure from yourself about being a writer. Allow your creativity to flow through you. There is a well of creativity within you that is so rich and full that it will never be empty. Trust yourself. *The Artist's Way, A Course in Discovering and Recovering Your Creative Self* by Julia Cameron is a wonderful book to help you get those creative juices flowing.

Go to a good nutritionist. There are many herbs you can take to strengthen your heart. Remember that your heart is a muscle, and it lovingly pumps joy throughout your body. As you relax in the evening, breathe deeply and affirm: MY HEART IS HEALTHY AND STRONG.

Dear Louise,

I am concerned about your position on the question of menopause and estrogen. Many women going through the transition endure terrible suffering, and they need the help of medical doctors and medication.

Also, I'm wondering about your feelings on estrogen therapy. We can naturally exist without estrogen, but with greatly diminished capacity. Why should any woman accept that? Childbirth, like menopause, is not a disease. Yet no woman today intentionally gives birth unattended at home. I agree that 'we, as women, are all divine and magnificent.' However, we should use our excellent minds to seek medical help when it is needed.

Dear One,

Thank you for sharing your views on these issues. As you point out, many women do experience terrible suffering as they move through menopause. This does not change the fact that menopause is a natural cycle of womanhood, nor does it mean that because some women suffer, that is the way it is supposed to be. Rather, I would choose to focus on the women who do not experience discomfort, and determine their attitudes and actions so that I may apply these to my own life.

More and more women today are choosing to take a more active, responsible role in their health care, to grow more in harmony with their bodies and allow processes of change such as menopause to unfold for them naturally, with little discomfort or diminished capacities. At the same time, for many of us, the level of responsibility and commitment to bring our minds and bodies into harmony surrounding deep-seated issues is too great. We need help from the medical profession or other sources until we feel ready or safe enough to confront some of the issues impacting our health and well-being, such as beliefs about self-worth. A far too common cultural belief, in our patriarchal society, is that women have little or no worth without their reproductive powers. Is it any wonder that many women fear and resist menopause? Estrogen therapy does not address these types of issues. Only our hearts and minds can heal these perceptions.

Does that mean I am condemning the medical profession for developing estrogen therapy as a means to cope with the dis-ease many women experience in menopause, or that I am finding fault with the women who take advantage of estrogen therapy? No. What I am suggesting is that striving for harmony and balance in our bodies and our minds can make potentially debilitating side-effect-ridden drug therapies unnecessary. We are discovering that natural progesterone is far more important to a woman's health than synthetic estrogen. Do read *Women's Bodies, Women's Wisdom* by Christiane Northrup, M.D. It is filled with wonderful information on how to keep a woman's body naturally

healthy. Affirm: I AM IN TUNE WITH MY INNER WIS-
DOM AND MOVE THROUGH LIFE HEALTHY, HAPPY,
AND WHOLE.

We are the pioneers who are working to change the old
negative belief patterns so that our daughters and our
daughters' daughters will never have to experience suffering
in menopause.

Dear Louise,

*You said we should forgive ourselves for things we did
wrong in the past, but what if you did something very
bad?*

*About seven years ago, I had an abortion. It seemed like the
best thing to do, and given who I was at that time, I did the
right thing. If the person I am now was faced with the same
decision, I'm sure I would make a different choice. If I try to
put this in the past and not think of it, I'm afraid that God
will think I'm unfeeling. I was raised to believe that bad deeds
would be punished at some point. I'm afraid that if I carry
this guilt around, something bad will happen. I would like to
have a child, but my husband won't come near me at all.
Could this be my punishment?*

Dear One,

You have determined in your own mind that the abortion you chose to have was something very bad. We all
make mistakes, and it's not the degree that we or society
puts on this mistake, but rather how we have chosen to be
unforgiving to ourselves. God has already forgiven you.
You are the one who is holding on to the guilt and letting
it keep you from living a happy, peaceful, and joyous life.
Let it go!

I don't think you are being punished by anyone or any-

213

Louise L. Hay

thing except yourself at this point. If you have felt undeserving of having a child or of having sex with your husband, you no doubt attracted a husband who will not come near you. If you change your thinking on abortion, you could have a chance of having a good sexual relationship with your husband.

A good affirmation for you could be: I FORGIVE MYSELF, AND THE HEALING HAS BEGUN.

Dear Louise,

I want to ask you about the right side of the body. It seems that any and all health problems I have are on my right side. I have neck pain, which goes down my right arm. I needed two teeth removed from the right side of my mouth. I found a lump on my right breast that looked like cancer, although it wasn't. I had my lymph nodes and one-quarter of my breast removed. Also, I had a hysterectomy, and my right ovary was removed.

What is the message? What is my lesson? Help!

Dear One,

The left side of the body is often regarded as the feminine side, the receiving side, where you take in. It represents, among other things, the mother. The right side of the body is often regarded as the masculine side, the giving-out side, where you express. It represents, among other things, the father. When we continually have problems with one particular side of the body, it can mean there are issues with the parent represented by the side that have not been settled. On some level, you may still be fighting with or giving in to your father. Even if it is only in your mind, you may still be giving him power over you.

Perhaps you can work with a therapist on these issues. If

214

that isn't possible, I suggest that you sit in front of a mirror (with a few tissues handy). Begin to talk to your father, just as though he were in the room, and tell him all the unresolved issues you have. When you are through, tell him you forgive him and you release him, that he is free and you are free. Whenever he passes through your mind or you have a problem with your body, just say, 'YOU ARE FREE. ALL IS WELL.'

Dear Louise,

I am writing to you because I have very painful breast cysts. My doctor has urged me to have a mammogram for six months now, but I have been too afraid.

Since I read your book You Can Heal Your Life, telling how you cured yourself of cancer, I keep thinking that if you did it with cancer, then I can do it with cysts. I just want to know if there are any other positive things I can be doing to complete my self-healing other than eating vegetables and fruits as much as possible.

Dear One,

I understand the concerns that you have about your breast cysts. My first recommendation, despite your fears, is for you to consult with your doctor. The pain in your body is a messenger; it is telling you that there is a condition that warrants your attention.

I applaud you for your willingness to work on changing your mental patterns, but at this point, I urge you to get the benefit of the information about your condition that your doctor will give you. God works through the medical profession, too. Do read everything you can get your hands on about the holistic methods of healing your condition. There is so much you can do for yourself in addition to what your doctor will do. Think of it as an act of loving the self. You may want to affirm: EVERY HAND THAT TOUCHES MY BODY IS A HEALING HAND, AND I AM SAFE.

Dear Louise,
I am a 32-year-old woman who is very, very hirsute. I have a mustache, and hair on my arms, breasts, stomach, and buttocks — and I literally get a five o'clock shadow on my legs after I shave them. I have as much hair on my body as a hairy man, and it is dark and coarse. I am neither overweight nor underweight, and I do not have any other physical 'abnormalities.'
My question is: Am I afraid of being female or of my womanliness so I unconsciously create a situation where I am uncomfortable with my body? Or should I think of my abnormal hair growth as a birth defect from which I must learn a life's lesson? Are there any affirmations I could use to heal my body and spirit? I am tired of feeling embarrassed. Thank you. I appreciate your being there for us.

Dear One,
I have personally known several women who have had to shave twice a day. In each case, they were extremely talented, creative people. Your hair growth is not abnormal for you. It means that you probably have lots of testosterone, which every woman has in differing amounts. Testosterone is supposed to increase energy and creativity, so it would be very helpful for you if you would consider yourself 'blessed' and use these gifts.

Each one of us grows up believing that there is something 'wrong' with us. This belief keeps us from being all that we can be. We each must learn to love ourselves in spite of what we consider a defect. There is no reason to feel embarrassed when you can help yourself. If you are uncomfortable with facial and body hair, visit a good electrologist. Nowadays, electrolysis is very effective and in time will permanently remove all unwanted hair.

Affirm: I AM BEAUTIFUL, AND EVERYBODY LOVES ME AS I AM. Say this affirmation at least 100 times a day for a month, and you will be amazed by the positive results.

Affirmations for Women

I see within myself a magnificent being.

I am discovering how wonderful I am.

I choose to love and enjoy myself.

I am wise and beautiful.

I love what I see in me.

I am in charge of my life.

I am free to be all I can be.

I stand on my own two feet.

I accept and use my own power.

I love, support, and enjoy the women in my life.

I am here to learn to love myself and to love other people unconditionally. Even though every person has measurable things about them, such as height and weight, there is far more to me than my physical expression. The immeasurable part of me is where my power is. Comparing myself with others makes me feel either superior or inferior, never acceptable exactly as I am. What a waste of time and energy. We are all unique, wonderful beings, each different and special. I go within and connect with the unique expression of eternal Oneness that I am and we all are.

Chapter Twenty

MISCELLANEOUS

W ho are you? Why are you here? What are your beliefs about life? For thousands of years, finding the answers to these questions has meant going within. But what does that mean?

I believe there is a Power within each of us that can lovingly direct us to our perfect health, perfect relationships, perfect careers, and which can bring us prosperity of every kind. In order to have those things, we have to believe first that they are possible. Next, we must be willing to release the patterns in our lives that are creating conditions we say we do not want. We do this by going within and tapping the Inner Power that already knows what is best for us. If we are willing to turn our lives over to this greater Power within, the Power that loves and sustains us, we can create more prosperous lives.

I believe that our minds are always connected to the One Infinite Mind; therefore, all knowledge and wisdom is available to us at any time. We are connected to this Infinite Mind, this Universal Power, through that spark of light within. The Universal Power loves all of Its creations. It is a Power for good, and It directs everything in our lives. It doesn't know how to hate or lie or punish. It is pure love, freedom, understanding, and compassion. It is important to turn our lives over to our Higher Self, because through It we receive our good.

We must understand that we have the choice to use this Power in any way we want. If we choose to live in the past and rehash all of the negative situations and conditions that went on way back when, then we stay stuck where we are. If we make a conscious decision not to be victims of the past and go about creating new lives for ourselves, we are supported by this Power within; and new, happier experiences begin to unfold.

We are each meant to be a wonderful, loving expression of life. Life is waiting for us to open up to it – to feel worthy of the good it holds for us. The wisdom and intelligence of the Universe is ours to use. Life is here to support us. We just need to trust the Power within to be there for us.

The following letters represent a variety of issues:

Dear Louise,

I would like some of your wonderful advice as to the outcome of the O. J. Simpson trial. I have been crying ever since the verdict. I want to believe that there is a reason for everything, but my heart hurts for the injustice. I feel for all women who have been abused and battered, and to think that women on the jury let him go. WHY?

There must be a divine plan to all of this. Our society is so angry and sick. Why can't we love one another? What good does all of the hatred, fear, and anger do? Yet, I am feeling it myself today.

Please send me a few words to help me understand what is happening in regards to Nicole, Ron, and all of us. I want so bad to believe that we can make a difference and the world can be healed of its pain and injuries.

Dear One,

I seldom read newspapers and have hardly followed the O. J. Simpson trial at all. I refuse to clutter my mind with most media turbulence. The media is good at stirring up our emotions and selling fear. If you read a newspaper from cover to cover every day, you will live in fear. They want you to buy a new paper each day to find out what to be afraid of that day. It is the same way with television news. If you want to sleep poorly, watch the late-night news just before you go to sleep. I will not buy into that. I cannot concentrate on helping to create a world where it is safe to love each other if I fill my mind with turbulence.

Not having been at the trial, nor having read about it, I cannot have any judgment about the outcome. I am sure that there are many things about this case that the public will never learn. I do know that everyone is under the law of their own consciousness and that what we give out will come back to us in some way. The murder of two people, as horrible as it is, has seemed to publicly uncover the even more horrendous, continual battering of helpless women and children. I have come to understand that out of every experience only good will come. If we focus our attention on bringing an end to the battering of all women, then good can come out of this experience.

Let's you and I, every time the thought of the trial comes to mind, say with conviction: THE WORLD IS BEING MADE A SAFE PLACE FOR ALL WOMEN AND CHILDREN, AND I AM CONTRIBUTING TO THAT SAFETY. We can make a difference. Your grieving period was fine. Now, use your powerful mind to help create the world we want to live in.

Dear Louise,
  After the bombings in Oklahoma and Saudi Arabia, the possible bombing of TWA flight 800, and the information I heard that three buildings in Phoenix were supposed to be bombed recently by fanatics, I can't help but be enraged by what I hear on the news. It scares me that people in our world can be so violent and malicious.

Louise L. Hay

What do you think is going to happen if this trend continues? Are you fearful for our country? I've never read your opinions on this subject, and I'm interested in what you have to say.

Dear One,

When people are raised in hatred, then terrorism seems natural to them. It is the ultimate act of blame. Blame is always a powerless act. It comes from believing that you have no control or responsibility over your circumstances. Those of us on the so-called path of enlightenment know that we are co-creators of our circumstances. Therefore, on some level, what is out there is a reflection of what we have within us. In order to heal the world, we need to heal the hatred in our own hearts. The best thing we can do is to work diligently to spread and share LOVE throughout the world. As we do this, we must realize that all that is *unloving* will come to the surface to be healed. We must look at and see the fear, hatred, racism, abuse, terrorism, and so on, in order to bring a new awareness to it. We cannot heal what we cannot or will not see.

We can see this as a frightening time, a time to let our own anger and rage emerge, or we can see these problems as opportunities to create healing. How *you choose* to use your mind is up to you. You can add to the problem or you can help heal it. When I hear of terrorist attacks or any crises in the world, I immediately surround the whole situation with white light. I send love and healing energy to everyone connected with it, including whomever may have done the damage. Rage and fear do not heal anything. Hatred begets hatred. An eye-for-an-eye philosophy makes everyone blind.

Let us all know and affirm: THINGS AREN'T GETTING WORSE; THEY ARE GETTING HEALED!

Dear Louise,

I am an 83-year-old widow, and I'm just fed up with life. I've raised a family, they live far away, and I'm all alone. Most of my friends have passed away. I wake up in the morning, eat breakfast, watch TV, and then sit around wondering what to do with myself. Please don't tell me to join a senior citizens' club or be a foster grandparent. I really have no interest. Anyway, I live in an outlying suburban area, and I can only get around by bus, so my mobility is limited.

To be honest, sometimes I just feel like ending it all, as I really feel that I don't have much to live for. I shudder to think that I might have to go on like this for another ten years or so. What advice do you have for someone like me?

Dear One,

You seem very clear on what you don't want. Have you given any thought as to what you really would like? If you could have anything you wanted, what would it be? How would you like to live the rest of your life? You have the opportunity before you to be a point of Light there in your hometown, sending out blessings to the entire Universe! And in doing so, those blessings return to you multiplied! Isn't that an awesome thought? I just read about seniors in Roanoke, Virginia, who are going back to school to learn how to use computers! What an incredible learning experience that could be for you to learn something new and exciting! Eighty-three is still young – I know of a 96-year-old woman who is the social director of her senior citizens' community! She is busy every day helping others. You are still here; you haven't left the planet yet. Enjoy your life. Be willing to receive new ways of thinking! Embrace the people in your life, and above all, love and appreciate the fact that you are who you are.

Learn to love yourself. Choose thoughts that make you

feel good. Only you can make yourself happy. The only place you can really live is in your mind. Affirm: MY LIFE IS JUST BEGINNING, AND I LOVE IT!

Dear Louise,

I am a very petite woman (4'3"), and people tell me that I am pretty. I have had a child, but I needed a Cesarean because I was too small for a natural birth. I deeply feel that my body has never developed to its full potential and that something is wrong with me. I feel very sad.

Is there any special reason why I chose a small body in this lifetime? If there is, how can I make the best of it? Are there any affirmations you can give me to move beyond this?

Dear One,

You might ask a basketball player why he chose a very tall body in this lifetime. Would you say that he has over-developed his potential and that something is wrong with him? He has as many challenges to living in this world as you do, only they are different. You both get to see life from a unique perspective.

Your body is not a problem; it is the way you have chosen to react to it. Your reaction is only a thought, and a thought can be changed. No matter what body we find ourselves in this time around, we want to rejoice in it.

If you don't love who you are, then you will teach your child the same feelings of worthlessness. I would suggest that both you and your child stand in front of a mirror and say: I LOVE MYSELF, I AM PERFECT JUST AS I AM. Do it every day. Make a song out of it. It will become a part of your being. All is well.

Dear Louise,

I am a happily married 27-year-old man who works in the engineering field. I like parts of my job, but I have a rather stressful relationship with my boss, since I do not really respect his judgment or his actions. However, this situation has been going on for over a year, and nothing has really changed recently, which is why I'm baffled by a physical problem that I've been having for the past two months.

I do get headaches periodically, anyway, but it seems that every Monday by about 2:00 P.M., I get a terrible migraine that lasts into the evening. I've been taking a prescription drug every Monday night when I come home from work, and I've come to dread that day each week because of these headaches. First, can you think of any reason why I might be having this problem on Mondays? And second, can you give me any advice on how to curtail them without using drugs?

Dear One,

Your body is telling you loud and clear to QUIT YOUR JOB! Why would you work for someone whom you do not respect at all? Of course you have migraines on Monday – you don't want to be there! You are forcing yourself to do something that violates your values, and then you punish yourself for doing so. More heart attacks occur on Monday morning than at any other time. Same reason: People hate their workplace.

Most people who create migraines are perfectionists. They stress out all week at work trying to be super-perfect, then when Friday night comes and they try to relax, all that tension bursts forth in a monumental migraine headache. Often, that headache will last all weekend. Your pattern is just a little different.

Love yourself enough to give yourself a 15-minute meditation break every day. Go somewhere on your lunch break. Sit quietly with your eyes closed, and for 15 minutes DO

227

NOTHING! You need to quiet yourself down inside. As you end your 'do nothing' period, use this affirmation: I ALWAYS WORK FOR WONDERFUL PEOPLE WHOM I RESPECT AND WHO RESPECT ME. Life will figure out how to make that true for you.

Dear Louise,

I am 23 years old, and after reading You Can Heal Your Life *several times, I still can't believe that we are responsible for what happens in our lives, because there has been no success in mine. My body doesn't work, my relationships don't work, my finances don't work — nothing works. How can I heal my life when I feel so bitter, frustrated, and angry toward the world?*

Dear One,

You are right. You cannot heal your life as long as you continue to create bitter, frustrated, and angry thoughts toward the world. What you give out will return to you as experiences. Bitter thoughts create more bitter experiences. Frustrated thoughts show that you have not yet learned your own responsibility in creating your world. Anger given out often returns as others being hurtful. I see that you are creating a world that perfectly matches your thoughts.

You have the power to continue to create chaos in your life, or you can release the negativity and begin to live life in a new and loving way. Yes, I do understand that you had a horrendous childhood. Someone somewhere in your early years taught you their own bitter outlook on life. You were a good child and learned it thoroughly. But now you are grown up, and you can form your own ideas about how you would like your life to be. Find a 12-step program to work with – any one could be good for you now. Read my book once more. This time do the exercises. Please say this affirmation several times a day for at least one month: I AM WILLING TO CHANGE. I AM WILLING TO LEARN TO LOVE MYSELF. Write this affirmation down and keep it near you at all times so that you can see it regularly.

You may not realize it now, but I know you are worth loving and that you can change your life for the better. As you release your negativity, you will begin to see your beauty, too.

Dear Louise,

Last June, the firm I worked for let 25 people go. After 23 years of loyalty and service, I received a package deal for which I am grateful. I've been happily married for 45 years and have children and grandchildren; however, I feel so lonely at times. I try to keep busy by helping others, but it doesn't seem to be enough. I feel that there is more to come for me, but I don't know what.

I have used affirmations to try to find a purpose in my life now, but I don't like waking up in the morning feeling that I don't have a destination. Am I trying too hard? I feel that I'm searching for 'more' in order to be happy within. Can you help me sort out these confused feelings?

Dear One,

You sound like a lady who feels useless unless you are working. I strongly suggest that you read the book *New Passages, Mapping Your Life Across Time* by Gail Sheehy. It is a brilliant book, beautifully written, and it addresses these very issues. Her insight into the New Map of Adult Life, and the possibility of changes that lie before us has touched a place in my heart. In 1900, our life expectancy was about 49

229

years. Today, people entering their 50s can easily live into their 90s. It is almost as though we are being given a second adulthood.

You, like many others today, are facing uncharted waters. Now that we are living longer, what does Life mean for us to do with all this extra time? We are entering a new evolutionary phase. We must prepare ourselves for new roles. Study something new. Go back to school. Be outrageous in your thinking. There is a whole new life ahead of you. I support you in exploring new worlds. Have fun. Do get any of the books by Sark – *Succulent Wild Woman* or *Inspiration Sandwich*. Both will inspire your creative freedom. Affirm: I AM OPEN AND RECEPTIVE TO NEW FULFILLMENT IN LIFE. ALL IS WELL!

Dear Louise,

Whenever I begin using affirmations, bad things start happening. You touched on this in your book You Can Heal Your Life – *how we'll affirm prosperity, then lose our wallet. Please expand on this as soon as possible, as I am getting discouraged. Thank you so much.*

Dear One,

Lots of us have so many negative messages in our subconscious mind that when we begin a program of positive self-improvement, we really stir up the pot, and all sorts of negative things come to the surface. I remember that in my early days, every time I did positive affirmations, I would hurt my body. This came from my old message of believing I deserved all the beatings I received as a child.

You will go beyond this period. Be very aware that this is just old stuff surfacing, and it cannot hurt you. Look at it in a positive way and say to yourself: 'This is only old junk coming to the surface. I am clearing it, and I am safe.' Also, give yourself a month of constantly forgiving everybody in your past with whom you have had problems. You might want to affirm in regard to each such person: I FORGIVE YOU, AND I SET YOU FREE. Remember, you deserve to be happy and free!

Dear Louise,

It has been pointed out to me that I preface all sentences with 'I guess.' I would like to stop this bad habit, but I am not even aware of doing it. I know that it means that somehow I am not sure of myself. What do you suggest?

Dear One,

The first thing you could do is to stop calling it a 'bad habit.' Please do not make yourself wrong because you want to improve the quality of your life. All of us are unsure of ourselves in some areas. Using repetitive expressions is common to many of us.

The fact that you have become aware of something you would like to change is the first step. Begin to listen to what you say. Conscious thinking is the goal we all want.

Use the affirmation: I AM A CLEAR THINKER, AND I EXPRESS MYSELF WITH EASE. And love yourself as you change.

Dear Louise,

I am a 36-year-old black woman who asks myself why some people of my own race act the way they do. At my job, they 'down' other races because of so-called facts put forth by other blacks, such as 'We are owed due to 400 years of oppression,'

231

'Other races are devils and only act nice to us,' 'Interracial mixing creates a new minority,' 'We have the right to be angry because things were taken from us,' 'No way am I dealing with anyone outside my race,' 'Black men suffer so much,' and so on. I'm sure you've heard it all.

I am fully aware of what has happened in the past, and I do see that racism still exists. Fear is the cause of this continuing hatred. I get along well with different races at my workplace, but the other blacks do not even care to try. I am made to feel that I 'kiss up' to my supervisor because I get the days off that I want and am commended for my work.

What is wrong with being myself; ridding myself of old, outdated beliefs; and eliminating negatives from my life? I have been doing affirmations regarding release, and I have been blessing my job with love and forgiveness.

Dear One,

As part of our journey in life, we are constantly learning lessons. Not all of us are ready to love all of life. Each person will change when the time comes for them to do so. It's easy to want to change everyone else's attitudes for the sake of the planet, but to judge another is self-righteous and delays our own growth. So just stay on your own pathway.

What you are doing is the best thing we all can do to heal the separation between all people. Continue to come from the loving space of your heart as much as you can, and don't pay attention to what others may say. Whenever you take a different position from the majority, you can expect to be ridiculed. I, too, get criticism from some people for my views on life, but I know that I must stick with what I believe.

What happened in the past with regard to racial matters is one of the most shameful parts of our nation's history. It is a wonder we did not have greater unrest much earlier. The prejudice and racism that continue to happen now are regrettable. They do not contribute to health and healing no matter who expresses them.

You are right when you say this hatred comes from fear. One day we will stop fearing each other and recognize that we are all one people, with the same capacity for loving and being loved.

Whenever you feel ridiculed by others for your beliefs, repeat this affirmation: I SEE HARMONY AND HEALING AMONG ALL PEOPLE EVERYWHERE. This will keep your focus on the vision you want.

Affirmations for Everyone

I am patient and kind with
all whom I encounter each day.

I am willing to see life in a new and different way.

I dwell in a world of love and acceptance.

I surround myself with positive people.

My dreams are a source of wisdom.

I ask for help when I need it.

I am willing to grow and change.

All that I have and all that I am is safe and secure.

I radiate acceptance, and I am deeply loved by others.

I constantly increase my awareness
of myself, my body, and my Life.

I LOVE MYSELF!

RECOMMENDED READING

Ageless Body, Timeless Mind – Deepak Chopra, M.D.
Aging Parents & You – Eugenia Anderson-Ellis
Alternative Medicine, the Definitive Guide – The Burton Goldberg Group
Anatomy of the Spirit: The Seven Stages of Power and Healing – Caroline Myss, Ph.D.
As Someone Dies – Elizabeth A. Johnson
Autobiography of a Yogi – Paramahansa Yogananda
Between Parent and Child – Hiam Ginott
The Canary and Chronic Fatigue – Majid Ali, M.D.
The Celestine Prophecy – James Redfield
The Complete Book of Essential Oils & Aromatherapy – Valerie Ann Worwood
Confidence: Finding It and Living It – Barbara De Angelis, Ph.D.
Constant Craving: What Your Food Cravings Mean and How to Overcome Them – Doreen Virtue, Ph.D.
The Contact Has Begun – Phillip H. Krapf
Cooking for Healthy Healing – Linda G. Rector-Page, N.D., Ph.D.
The Course in Miracles – Foundation for Inner Peace
Creative Visualization – Shakti Gawain
Diet for a New America – John Robbins
Discovering the Child Within – John Bradshaw
Do What You Love, the Money Will Follow – Marsha Sinetar
Everyday Wisdom – Dr. Wayne Dyer
Feel the Fear and Do It Anyway – Susan Jeffers, Ph.D.
Fire in the Soul – Joan Borysenko, Ph.D.

237

Fit for Life – Harvey and Marilyn Diamond
A God Who Looks Like Me – Patricia Lynn Reilly
Great American Cookbook – Marilyn Diamond
Growing Older, Growing Better – Amy E. Dean
Healing the Heart, Healing the Body – Ron Scolastico, Ph.D.
Healthy Healing, An Alternative Healing Reference – Linda
    G. Rector-Page, N.D., Ph.D.
The Heroic Path: One Woman's Journey from Cancer to Self-
    Healing – Angela Passidomo Trafford
How to Meditate – Lawrence LeShan
'I'd Change My Life If I Had More Time' – Doreen Virtue,
    Ph.D.
Lighten Up (audiocassette) – Carol Hansen (Open Heart
    Productions: 510–974–9088)
Instead of Therapy: Help Yourself Change and Change the
    Help You're Getting – Tom Rusk, M.D.
Learning to Love Yourself – Sharon Wegscheider-Cruse
Life After Life – Raymond Moody, M.D.
Lifegoals – Amy E. Dean
Life! You Wanna Make Something of It? – Tom Costa, M.D.
Losing Your Pounds of Pain: Breaking the Link Between
    Abuse, Stress, and Overeating – Doreen Virtue, Ph.D.
Love Is Letting Go of Fear – Gerald Jampolsky, M.D.
Love, Medicine, and Miracles – Bernie Siegel, M.D.
The Menopause Industry: How the Medical Establishment
    Exploits Women – Sandra Coney
Minding the Body, Mending the Mind – Joan Borysenko, Ph.D.
Mutant Message, Down Under – Marlo Morgan
My Mother Made Me Do It – Nan Kathryn Fuchs
New Passages: Mapping Your Life Across Time – Gail Sheehy
Opening Our Hearts to Men – Susan Jeffers, Ph.D.
Parents' Nutrition Bible – Dr. Earl Mindell, R.Ph., Ph.D.
Peace, Love & Healing – Bernie Siegel, M.D.
The Power of the Mind to Heal – Joan and Miroslav
    Borysenko, Ph.D.s
The Power of Touch – Phyllis K. Davis

Prescription for Nutritional Healing – James F. Balch, M.D.;
and Phyllis A. Balch, C.N.C.
Real Magic – Dr. Wayne W. Dyer
Reinventing Womanhood – Carolyn Heilbrun
The Relaxation Response – Benson and Klipper
A Return to Love – Marianne Williamson
Revolution from Within – Gloria Steinem
Saved by the Light – Dannion Brinkley
Self-Parenting – John Pollard III
Staying on the Path – Dr. Wayne W. Dyer
Super Nutrition Gardening – Dr. William S. Peavy and
Warren Peary
*Take Back Your Power: A Working Woman's Response to
Sexual Harassment* – Jennifer Coburn
Thoughts of Power and Love – Susan Jeffers, Ph.D.
The Tibetan Book of Living and Dying – Sogyal Rinpoche
The Western Guide to Feng Shui – Terah Kathryn Collins
What Do You Really Want for Your Children? – Dr. Wayne
W. Dyer
*What Every Woman Needs to Know Before (and After) She
Gets Involved with Men and Money* – Judge Lois Forer
When 9 to 5 Isn't Enough – Marcia Perkins-Reed
*Woman Heal Thyself: An Ancient Healing System for
Contemporary Woman* – Jeanne Elizabeth Blum
A Woman's Worth – Marianne Williamson
Women Alone: Creating a Joyous and Fulfilling Life – Julie
Keene and Ione Jenson
Women's Bodies, Women's Wisdom (as well as her audios
and her newsletter, *Health Wisdom for Women*) –
Christiane Northrup, M.D.
Women Who Love Too Much – Robin Norwood
Your Sacred Self – Dr. Wayne W. Dyer

* Any book by Emmett Fox or Dr. John MacDonald
* Also, the audiocassette program, *Making Relationships
Work* by Barbara De Angelis, Ph.D.

SELF-HELP RESOURCES

The following list of resources can be used for more information about recovery options for addictions, health concerns, death and bereavement, and other issues. The addresses and telephone numbers listed are for the national headquarters; look in your local yellow pages for resources closer to your area.

In addition to the following groups, other self-help organizations may be available in your area to assist your healing and recovery for a particular life crisis not listed here. Consult your telephone directory, or call a counseling center or help line near you.

AIDS

AIDS Education and
  Research Fund (AVERT)
11–13 Denne Parade
Horsham, W. Sussex
tel 01403 210202

Children with Aids Charity
2nd floor, 111 High
  Holborn,
London WC1V 6JS
tel 0171 242 3883

London Lighthouse
111–117 Lancaster Road
London W11 1QT
tel 0171 792 1200

National AIDS helpline
PO Box 5000
Glasgow G12 9JQ
tel 0141 357 1774

Terrence Higgins Trust Ltd
52–54 Gray's Inn Road
London WC1X 8JU
tel 0171 831 0330
Helpline 0171 242 1010

Louise L. Hay

ALCOHOL ABUSE

Al-Anon
61 Great Dover Street
London SE1 4YF
tel 0171 403 0888

Alcohol and Drug
    Addiction Prevention
    and Treatment Limited
    (ADAPT)
6 Langley St.
London WC2H 9JA
tel 0171 240 4026;
fax 0171 240 4027

Alcohol Concern
Waterbridge House
32–36 Loman St.
London SE1 OEE
tel 0171 928 7377

Alcohol Education and
    Research Council
Room 143, Horseferry
    House,
Dean Ryle Street
London SW1P 2AW
tel 0171 217 8393;
fax 0171 217 8799

Alcohol Problems Advisory
    Service
Local Call Rate Linkline
    0345 626316

Alcoholics Anonymous
PO Box 1
Stonebow House, Stonebow
York, YO1 7NJ
tel 01904 644026

ANOREXIA BULIMIA

Anorexia Anonymous
24 Westmoreland Road,
Barnes
London SW13
tel 0181 748 3994

Eating Disorders, The
    Maisner Centre for
PO Box 464
Hove, E. Sussex, BN3 2BN
tel 01273 729818

CANCER

Cancer and Leukemia in
    Childhood (CLIC)
CLIC Headquarters
12/13 King Square
Bristol BS2 8JH
tel 0117 924 8844;
fax 0117 924 4505

Cancer Care Society
39 The Hundred
Romsey, Hampshire
SO51 8GE
tel 01794 830374;
fax 01794 518133

Cancer Research Campaign
10 Cambridge Terrace
London NW1 4JL
tel 0171 224 1333;
fax 0171 487 4310

CHILDREN'S ISSUES

Child Bereavement Trust
Harleyford Estate
Henley Road, Marlow
Buckinghamshire, SL7 2DX
tel and fax 01628 488101

Child Health Research
  Appeal Trust
Institute of Child Health
30 Guilford St., London
  WC1N 1EH
tel 0171 242 9789;
fax 0181 829 8689

Childline
2nd Floor, Royal Mail
  Building
Studd St., London
  N1 OQW
tel 0171 239 1000 (office);
  freephone 0800 1111
fax 0171 239 1001

Children in Crisis
4 Calico House,
London SW11 3UB
tel 0171 978 5001;
fax 0171 978 5003

Children's Society
Edward Rudolf House
59–85 Margery St.,
London WC1X OJL
tel 0171 837 4299

Incest:
Rainer Foundation
89 Blackheath Hill
London SE10 8JJ
tel 0181 694 9497

PCCA-Christian Child Care
PO Box 133, Swanley, Kent
  BR8 7UQ
tel 01322 660011;
fax 01322 614788

Tower Hamlets Youth
  Counselling Service
Oxford House
Derbyshire St.
London E2 6HG
tel 0171 739 3082

Louise L. Hay

DEATH/GRIEVING/ SUICIDE

CRUSE Bereavement Care
Cruse House, 126 Sheen
  Road
Richmond, Surrey
  TW9 1UR
tel 0181 940 4818

Samaritans *see* local
  telephone directory

Child Bereavement Trust
  see under **CHILDREN'S
  ISSUES**

DEBTS

Citizens Advice Bureau
See local telephone directory

National Debt Helpline
0121 359 8501

DIABETES

Action Research
Vincent House, Horsham
W. Sussex, RH12 2DP
tel 01403 210406;
fax 01403 210541

British Diabetic Association
10 Queen Anne St.
London W1M OBD
tel 0171 323 1531; fax 0171
  636 3096

DRUG ABUSE

Alcohol and Drug
  Addiction Prevention
  and Treatment Limited
  (ADAPT)
6 Langley St.
London WC2H 9JA
tel 0171 240 4026;
fax 0171 240 4027

Drug & Alcohol
  Counselling Service
  (DACS)
48 Oswald Rd, Scunthorpe
tel 01724 854763;
fax 01724 271682

Release
National Drugs and Legal
  Services
388 Old St.
London EC1V 9LT
daytime helpline 10 am-6 pm
  0171 729 9904
*overnight and weekend
  helpline* 0171 603 8654
administration 0171 729 5255

EATING DISORDERS

Eating Disorders
Scottish Centre
3 Sciennes Rd.
Edinburgh EH9 1LE
tel 0131 668 3051

Eating Disorders
    Association
Sackville Place
44 Magdalen St.
Norwich NR3 1JE
tel 01603 621414

GAMBLING

Gamblers Anonymous and
    Gam-Anon
PO Box 88
London SW19 0EU
tel 0171 384 3040
see also local telephone directory

HEALTH ISSUES

Health Unlimited
Prince Consort House
27–29 Albert Embankment
London SE1 7TS
tel 0171 582 5999

Alzheimer's Disease

Alzheimer's Disease Society
Gordon House
10 Greencoat Place
London SW1P 1PH
tel 0171 306 0606

Arthritis

Arthritis Care
18 Stephenson Way
London NW1 2HD
tel 0171 916 1500
Freephone helpline
0800 289170

Back Pain

National Back Pain
    Association
16 Elmtree Rd.
Teddington
Middx TW11 BST
0181 977 5474

Epilepsy

National Society for
    Epilepsy (NSE)
Chalfont St Peter
Gerrards Cross
Bucks SL9 0RJ
tel 01494 601300

Fertility

ISSUE (The National
  Fertility Association)
509 Aldridge Rd.
Great Barr
Birmingham B44 8NA
tel 0121 344 4414

Health Information

Healthline
St Margaret's House
21 Old Ford Rd.
London E2 9PL
tel 0181 983 1553

Holistic Medicine

British Holistic Medical
  Association
The Royal Shrewsbury
  Hospital South
Shrewsbury SY3 8XF
tel 01743 261155

Hospices

Hospice Information
  Service
St Christopher's Hospice
51–59 Lawrie Park Rd.
London SE26 6DZ
tel 0181 778 9252

Mental Health

MIND (The National
  Association for Mental
  Health)
Granta House
15–19 Broadway
Stratford
London E15 4BQ
tel 0181 519 2122

Migraine

British Migraine
  Association
178a High Rd.
Byfleet
Surrey KT14 7ED
tel 01932 352468

Multiple Sclerosis

Multiple Sclerosis Society
25 Effie Rd.
Fulham
London SW6 1EE
tel 0171 610 7171
helpline 0171 371 8000

Strokes

The Stroke Association
CHSA House
Whitecross St.
London EC1Y 8JJ

HOMELESSNESS

Centrepoint
Bewlay House
2 Swallow Place
London W1R 7AA
tel 0171 629 2229

Homes for Homeless
People
6 Union St.
Luton
Bedfordshire LU1 3AN
tel 01582 481426

INCEST

Rainer Foundation
89 Blackheath Hill
London SE10 8JJ
tel 0181 694 9497

ICAIRR (Independent Care
After Incestuous Relation-
ship and Rape)
Gatehouse
Whiteways
Great Chesterfield
Essex CB10 1NX
tel 01799 530520

RAPE

Edinburgh Rape Crisis
Centre
PO Box 120
Brunswick Rd.
Edinburgh EH7 5XX
tel 0131 556 9437

Rape Crisis Centre
PO Box 69
London WC1X 9NJ
tel 0171 916 5466; 0171 837
1600

Wearside Women in Need
1st Floor, The Elms
Concord
Washington
Tyne & Wear NE37 2BA
tel 0191 416 3550

SMOKING ABUSE

Action on Smoking and
Health (ASH)
109 Gloucester Place
London W1H 3PH
tel 0171 935 3519

Louise L. Hay

SPOUSE ABUSE

Women Against Violent
  Spouses (WAVE)
37 Church St.
Heage
Derbyshire DE56 2BG
tel 01773 852857

THERAPY

The Women's Therapy
  Centre
6/9 Manor Gardens
London N7 6LA
tel 0171 263 6200

SELF-HELP RESOURCES IN SOUTH AFRICA

AIDS

ATIC – AIDS Training and Information Centre
(011) 7256720

AIDS Centre
(011) 7256710

ALCOHOL ABUSE

Alcoholics Anonymous
8 Unity Centre
260 Louis Botha Ave
Johannesburg
(011) 4832470

Al-Anon Family Service
Asklipeon Centre
Albert Street
Johannesburg
(011) 4359792

Riverfield Lodge Alcohol-
ism & Drug Dependency
PO Box 539
Randburg
(011) 4601970

CANCER

Cancer Association of
South Africa
26 Concord Road
Bedford View
(011) 6167662

CHILDREN'S ISSUES

Child Abuse Action Group
PO Box 1153
Houghton
(011) 7935033

Child Abuse Alliance
PO Box 29177
Sandringham
(011) 4853350

Johannesburg Child
  Welfare Society
Liberty Life Centre
Main Street
Johannesburg
3311303

Childline
Toll Free – 0800055555

DEATH/GRIEVING/
SUICIDE

Nechama Bereavement
  Counselling
Granville Court
Grafton Road
Yeoville
(011) 4871208

DEBT

Legalwise
Goldman Street
Johannesburg
(011) 4704000

Citizen's Advice Bureau
City Hall
Market Street
Johannesburg
8360817

Department of Labour
Annity House
Rissik Street
Johannesburg
(011) 4973000

DIABETES

Diabetes Association of
  South Africa
143 Admirals Court
Rosebank
(011) 4476265

DRUG ABUSE

Nar Anon
(011) 8643389
Meetings at Hillbrow
Recreation Centre

Narcotics Anonymous
(011) 4407073

EATING
DISORDERS

Overeaters Anonymous
PO Box 46206
Orange Grove
(011) 6402901

Phone A Friend
Counselling & Practical
Advice for Sufferers of
Anorexia & Bulimia
33 Algernon Road
Norwood, 2192
(011) 7284698

FAMILY HEALTH

Family Life Centre
His Majesty's Building
Commissioner's Street
(011) 8832057

Family Planning Clinic
Johannesburg Hospital
Jubilee Road
Parktown
(011) 4843498

HEALTH ISSUES

Asthma

National Asthma Education
    Programme
PO Box 72128
Parkview
2122

Arthritis

Arthritis Foundation
Medical School
York Road
Parktown
Johannesburg
(011) 6472131

Epilepsy

Reea Epilepsy Centre
(011) 7884745

Headaches

Headache Clinic
179A Jan Smuts Avenue
Parktown North
(011) 8806464

Holistic Medicine

South African College of
    Natural Therapies
71 Charl Cilliers Avenue
Alberton North
(011) 9078818

Bella Vita Clinic
103 Central Street
Hougton
(011) 7283996

Louise L. Hay

Hospices

Hospice Association of
    Witwatersrand
PO Box 87600
Hougton
(011) 4831068

Mental Health

Mental Health Society
(011) 6242344

Multiple Sclerosis

South African National
    Multiple Sclerosis
Society
PO Box 317, Melville
(011) 7267494

INCEST

Support Group for Adult
    Survivors
Contact: Follies Spies
(021) 4296656

RAPE

Rape Crisis
(011) 4872743

SPOUSE ABUSE

PAWA: People Against
    Women Abuse
(011) 6424345

Women Against Woman
    Abuse
(011) 8365656

Women's Bureau
(011) 3481232

Advice Desk for Abused
    Women
(031) 8202860

HELP LINES

Flying Squad
10111 – Nationwide

Ambulance Service
999 – Nationwide

Suicide Helpline
4032626

Lifeline
(011) 7281347
0800012322 – toll free

TRAUMA SERVICES

WITS Trauma Clinic
Counselling For Victims of
  Violence
(011) 4035102

Trauma Unit for Victims of
  Violence of Hijacking
(011) 4035102

ABOUT THE AUTHOR

LOUISE L. HAY is a metaphysical lecturer and teacher and the bestselling author of 20 books including *You Can Heal Your Life* and *Empowering Women*. Her works have been translated into 25 different languages in 33 countries throughout the world. Since beginning her career as a Science of Mind minister in 1981, Louise has assisted thousands of people in discovering and using the full potential of their own creative powers for personal growth and self-healing.

BOOKS, AUDIOS, AND VIDEOS BY
LOUISE L. HAY

Books

The Aids Book: Creating a Positive Approach
Colors & Numbers
Empowering Women
A Garden of Thoughts: My Affirmation Journal
Gratitude: A Way of Life (Louise and Friends)
Heal Your Body
Heal Your Body A-Z
Heart Thoughts: A Treasury of Inner Wisdom
Letters to Louise
Life! Reflections on Your Journey
Love Your Body
Love Yourself, Heal Your Life Workbook
Loving Thoughts for Health and Healing
Loving Thoughts for Increasing Prosperity
Loving Thoughts for a Perfect Day
Loving Thoughts for Loving Yourself
Meditations to Heal Your Life
101 Power Thoughts
The Power Is Within You
You Can Heal Your Life

Coloring Books/Audiocassettes for Children

Lulu and the Ant: A Message of Love
Lulu and the Dark: Conquering Fears
Lulu and Willy the Duck: Learning Mirror Work

Audiocassettes

Aids: A Positive Approach
Cancer: Discovering Your Healing Power
Elders of Excellence
Empowering Women
Feeling Fine Affirmations
Gift of the Present *with Joshua Leeds*
Heal Your Body (Audio Book)
Life! Reflections on Your Journey (Audio Book)
Love Your Body (Audio Book)
Loving Yourself

Meditations for Personal Healing
Meditations to Heal Your Life (Audio Book)
Morning and Evening Meditations
Overcoming Fears
The Power Is Within You (Audio Book)
Self Healing
Songs of Affirmation *with Joshua Leeds*
What I Believe/Deep Relaxation
You Can Heal Your Life (Audio Book)
You Can Heal Your Life Study Course

Conversations on Living Lecture Series

Change and Transition
Dissolving Barriers
The Forgotten Child Within
How to Love Yourself
The Power of Your Spoken Word
Receiving Prosperity
Totality of Possibilities
Your Thoughts Create Your Life

Personal Power Through Imagery Series

Anger Releasing
Forgiveness/Loving the Inner Child

Subliminal Mastery Series

Feeling Fine Affirmations
Love Your Body Affirmations
Safe Driving Affirmations
Self-Esteem Affirmations
Self-Healing Affirmations
Stress-Free Affirmations

Videocassettes

Dissolving Barriers
Doors Opening: A Positive Approach to Aids
Receiving Prosperity
You Can Heal Your Life Study Course
Your Thoughts Create Your Life

Available at your local bookstore, or call:

**(001) 800–654–5126 or
(001) 760–431–7695**

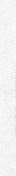